Getting Started in

HEDGE FUNDS

D1417674

The *Getting Started In* Series

Getting Started in Online Day Trading by Kassandra Bentley
Getting Started in Investment Clubs by Marsha Bertrand
Getting Started in Asset Allocation by Bill Bresnan and Eric P. Gelb
Getting Started in Online Investing by David L. Brown and Kassandra Bentley
Getting Started in Online Brokers by Kristine DeForge
Getting Started in Internet Auctions by Alan Elliott
Getting Started in Stocks by Alvin D. Hall
Getting Started in Mutual Funds by Alvin D. Hall
Getting Started in Estate Planning by Kerry Hannon
Getting Started in Online Personal Finance by Brad Hill
Getting Started in 401(k) Investing by Paul Katzeff
Getting Started in Internet Investing by Paul Katzeff
Getting Started in Security Analysis by Peter J. Klein
Getting Started in Global Investing by Robert P. Kreitler
Getting Started in Futures by Todd Lofton
Getting Started in Project Management by Paula Martin and Karen Tate
Getting Started in Financial Information by Daniel Moreau and Tracey Longo
Getting Started in Emerging Markets by Christopher Poillon
Getting Started in Technical Analysis by Jack D. Schwager
Getting Started in Hedge Funds by Daniel A. Strachman
Getting Started in Options by Michael C. Thomsett
Getting Started in Six Sigma by Michael C. Thomsett
Getting Started in Real Estate Investing by Michael C. Thomsett and Jean Freestone Thomsett
Getting Started in Tax-Savvy Investing by Andrew Westham and Don Korn
Getting Started in Annuities by Gordon M. Williamson
Getting Started in Bonds by Sharon Saltzgiver Wright
Getting Started in Retirement Planning by Ronald M. Yolles and Murray Yolles
Getting Started in Currency Trading by Michael D. Archer and Jim L. Bickford
Getting Started in Rental Income by Michael C. Thomsett

Getting Started in

HEDGE FUNDS

SECOND EDITION

Daniel A. Strachman

WILEY

John Wiley & Sons, Inc.

For general information on our other products and services, or technical support, please
contact our Customer Care Department within the United States at 800-762-2974, outside
the United States at 317-572-3993 or fax 317-572-4002.

Wiley also publishes its books in a variety of electronic formats. Some content that appears
in print may not be available in electronic books. For more information about Wiley
products, visit our web site at www.wiley.com.

ISBN-13 978-0-471-71544-3
ISBN-10 0-471-71544-1

Printed in the United States of America

10 9 8 7 6 5 4 3 2 1

To My Wife, Felice,
and My Daughter, Leah

Contents

Acknowledgments   ix

Introduction

    Why Hedge Funds?   1

Chapter 1

    Hedge Fund Basics   9

        The Near Collapse of Long-Term
          Capital Management   13

        A Brief History of Hedge Funds   25

        The Current State of the Hedge Fund Industry   31

        Alfred Winslow Jones—The Original Hedge
          Fund Manager   33

Chapter 2

    How Hedge Funds Operate   45

        Starting a Hedge Fund   48

        Hedge Fund Regulations and Structures   67

        How Hedge Funds Use Leverage   78

        Patriarchs of the Hedge Fund World   80

        Hedge Funds Take All the Heat   85

        George Soros—The World's Greatest Investor   90

Chapter 3

    The Managers   93

        Judy Finger and Doug Topkis—Haystack Capital LP   96

        David Taylor and Mike Williams—Cover Asset
          Management LLC   102

Paul Reiferson and Jeff Lopatin—Americus
    Partners LP   108
Guy Wyser-Pratte—Wyser-Pratte   113
Bill Michaelcheck—Mariner Investment Group   123
Nancy Havens-Hasty—Havens Advisors LLC   131
Steve Cohen—SAC Capital   138

Chapter 4

Hedge Fund Investing   **145**
    An Investment Adviser   147
    An Institutional Investor   151
    Third-Party Marketers   156
    An Individual Investor   161
    A Consulting Firm   165
    A Manager of Managers   168

Conclusion   **175**

Appendix
    Hedge Fund Strategies   **179**

Glossary   **187**

Notes   **189**

Index   **193**

Acknowledgments

The idea for the first edition of this book came to me in the mid-1990s while working at Cantor Fitzgerald and, as a result of a number of unique events, the book became a reality in 2000. Now Wiley is publishing a second edition. Over the past year or so, I have tried to update the pages of this book to make it as relevant as possible for those interested in learning more about hedge funds and the hedge fund industry. I hope that you, the reader, find it worthwhile and, more importantly, worthy of your time. Your interest in hedge funds has made this book possible, and I thank you very much for your interest in this fascinating subject.

Like it or not, hedge funds are here to stay. As an investment vehicle they are no longer considered an alternative investment but rather an important investment in a diversified portfolio. And although hedge funds have not yet become "traditional," in the months and years ahead the differences that separate traditional investments and hedge funds are going to become smaller and smaller. Hedge funds are not going anywhere because people understand the value of creating a portfolio that is hedged against market volatility. Hedge funds are for investors of all shapes and sizes and play an important role in the future of the financial markets. Hedge funds are important and are finally getting the respect they deserve.

To write this book I called on many of the usual suspects who have helped me over the years to make me look good in print. Without their help, I probably would not have been able to complete this project. They are of course Viki Goldman, the greatest librarian and researcher I have ever met and Sam Graff, the only true newspaper man left in the tri-state area. Thank you for the hard work you always contribute to make my work better. I truly appreciate it.

The people at Wiley have once again provided a platform for my work and to all of them, I say thank you. I hope the book is all you intended it to be when you gave me the go-ahead to write it.

I want to thank my family for their support and guidance over the years. It is through your efforts that this book is possible.

And finally to Felice, all I can say is thank you for being a provider of inspiration and support to see this project through.

DANIEL A. STRACHMAN

New York, New York
June 2005

Why Hedge Funds?

In the past eight years, hedge funds have gone from relative obscurity to being a topic of cocktail party chatter and reports on the evening news.

Hedge funds and those who manage and invest in them have become the most talked about investment since the Internet initial public offerings (IPOs). The rise from obscurity began with the astronomical returns that many hedge funds posted during the euphoria that has swept the investment world in recent years. Now, the interest has been sparked by the opposite: losses racked up in the past few years by many of the hedge fund world's most famous and sought-after managers. At the beginning of the new millennium, the issues for investors were "How do I invest?" and "How much can I expect?" At the halfway point of the decade the issues had become "How do I get my money out?" and "Is there anything left?" After the technology bubble burst and investors realized that there was more to making money in the markets than simply buying companies with .com in their name, they began to look to alternatives. In this case the alternative happened to be the hedge fund. Why did they look to hedge

1

funds for returns? The answer is the same as that given by Willie Horton when he was asked why he robbed banks—because that's where the money is. Unlike the technology bubble that lasted a mere three years, the hedge fund craze is here to stay. Once again, the greed that was deemed good in the 1980s is back in favor among investors. However, today instead of hoping to ride the tails of takeover artists, investors are looking to hedge fund managers for the returns they so desperately crave.

Over the years, hedge fund managers, like most money managers as a group, have experienced their ups and downs. In the late 1990s and the early part of 2000, many of the investment world's biggest and brightest stars posted significant losses and in some cases were forced to liquidate their hedge funds. Today as then investors do not want to believe that these so-called Midas traders could make such drastic mistakes and run into so much trouble. Since the initial stories broke, the markets have turned for the better. As can be expected, some funds were able to stop the hemorrhaging, having been left with significantly less money under management. Others have seen their funds grow by leaps and bounds. In the midst of the carnage many pundits believed that the hedge fund business was finished. The truth is exactly the opposite. Hedge funds are here to stay. Sure, some may be wiped out or close their doors voluntarily, but there will always be someone else willing to open another hedge fund.

prime broker service offered by major brokerage firms providing clearance, settlement, trading, and custody functions for hedge funds.

Not only are hedge funds thriving, the *prime brokers*, administrators, lawyers, and accountants who service them are, too. The reason? Wall Street is about making money—and running a hedge fund provides one of the greatest ways to do it.

This book is intended to provide an overview of the hedge fund industry. It covers many of the most important subjects surrounding running and investing in these investment vehicles. Certainly there is no one way to invest in hedge funds, as there are so many different funds with just as many different investment strategies and philosophies. A key goal of this book is to provide an objective view of the industry, one that gives you an understanding of the complex world of hedge funds that has dramatically changed since the concept was created in the late 1940s.

The growing importance and impact of hedge funds make it a subject that all investors should seek to understand. That's especially true because there are so many misconceptions about the industry.

Today, many people outside Wall Street believe that Long-Term Capital Management LP and George Soros are the sole representatives of the entire hedge fund industry. This is just not the case. Although it is difficult to give an exact number, at last count there were more than 8,000 hedge funds with roughly $850 billion under management. While the Soros organization is generally considered to be the most famous hedge fund manager and Long-Term Capital is probably the most notorious hedge fund organization, they are a far cry from representing the entire industry. The industry stretches all over the world and ranges from men and women who manage titanic sums of money to those who manage a relative pittance.

The common perception is quite different from reality. The perception of the hedge fund world is that of gunslingers and traders who manage billions of dollars by the seat of their pants. The reality is that most hedge funds have far less than $100 million under management and, in most cases, every single trade that is executed is a calculated move. But no matter how often or how much the managers talk to the press, they can't seem to shed the stigma of being gunslingers. A careful look, however, will show there is probably more risk to investing in an ordinary mutual fund than in most hedge funds because hedge funds are able to go both long and short the market. Mutual fund managers are generally only able to go one way—long the market, which means that should the market enter a prolonged period of negative returns it will be extremely difficult for the mutual fund to put up positive numbers—whereas a hedge fund manager can take advantage of the downside by going short. Another critical difference between hedge funds and mutual funds that in my opinion makes them less risky is that in most cases, hedge fund managers put all of their own capital into their own fund. In short, they put their money where their mouths are. The losses or gains directly affect the size of their own bank accounts along with those of their investors.

People who think that hedge funds are run by ruthless men and women looking to make a buck at any cost do not understand the basic concept of hedge fund management. Although a few managers may operate in this fashion, most do not. Most are interested in two things: preserving capital and making money for their partners. The hedge fund industry is a stay-rich business—not a get-rich business. If you ask managers what is the most important aspect of their business, they will tell you: the preservation of capital. It takes money to make money. If you lose capital, you limit your resources to invest further and you soon will be out of business. By limiting risk and not betting the ranch on a single investment, they will live to invest another day. For hedge fund managers, slow and steady wins the race. The men and women who run hedge funds are some of the most dedicated money managers in the world. This dedication shows in their ability to continually outperform the market.

There is a big difference between hedge funds and mutual funds. The first is the size of the industry. The largest hedge fund complex has less than $20 billion in assets under management while the largest mutual fund has more than $100 billion in assets under management. All mutual funds are highly regulated by the Securities and Exchange Commission (SEC) and are open to any and all investors, assuming they can meet the minimum investment requirements. Hedge funds are not open to the general public, only to accredited investors and institutions. Accredited investors as defined by the SEC are individuals who have a net worth of a million dollars or who have had net income of $200,000 in the past two years and have reasonable expectations of continued income at that level. Hedge funds are not allowed to advertise.

The SEC does not allow mutual fund managers to use *derivatives* or to sell securities short to enhance performance. Hedge funds can use any legal means necessary to produce results. Most mutual fund managers are paid on the basis of the amount of assets they attract, while hedge fund managers are paid for performance. Unlike mutual fund investing, hedge fund investing is about calculating how to perform in good and bad markets through the use of investment strategies that consist of *long positions* and *short positions*. Whereas mutual fund managers are limited to taking long positions in stocks and bonds, hedge fund managers are able to use a much more extensive array of investment strategies such as the use of shorting and derivatives. It is all about capital preservation and healthy returns.

In the large hedge fund complexes, accountability for the funds rests with multiple managers, analysts, and traders. In smaller organizations, a single individual is accountable for the funds. Most hedge fund organizations usually consist of a small staff working with the manager. While the size and scope of the organizations vary, all hedge funds seek to provide investors with a valuable service: capital preservation mixed with healthy returns. The common theme among all hedge fund managers is to use investment strategies that create a diversified portfolio that over time will outperform the market regardless of market conditions.

derivatives
securities that take their values from another security.

long position
a transaction to purchase shares of a stock resulting in a net positive position.

short position
a transaction to sell shares of stock that the investor does not own.

The purpose of this book is to provide an introduction that explores these types of operations. I purposely did not examine managers and funds that are covered in the popular press. Instead I spent time getting to know managers who are known on Wall Street but not outside it. They manage portfolios ranging in size from $2 million to over $2 billion. In some cases they operate by themselves out of a small office with one assistant. Others have multiple offices around the globe with staffs of a hundred or more.

The idea of the book is to provide you with a clearer view at how these people operate in the various markets that they trade. Because each employs different trading methodologies and investment philosophies, this book provides you with a unique look at the business of managing money. It will, I hope, give you the insight you need to find alternative means to achieve your investment goals. While all the managers are different, they all have two things in common: They use some piece of the same business model and each is an entrepreneur.

While profiles of managers make up a significant portion of this book, other pages describe the history of the industry and how it has evolved. George Soros, Michael Steinhardt, and Julian Robertson, unlike what many have been led to believe, did not create the hedge fund industry. They may have advanced the concept, but the idea and the term were created by journalist Alfred Winslow Jones, a visionary who used his knowledge of sociology and his reporting skills to come up with the idea in the late 1940s while researching an article for *Fortune* magazine.

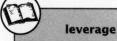

leverage means of enhancing return or value without increasing investment. Buying securities on margin is an example of leverage.

Jones's basic concept is simple: By combining the use of long and short positions coupled with the use of *leverage*, a manager should be able to outperform the market in good times and to limit losses in bad times. Today most hedge funds employ the same concept. Like everything else, however, each manager uses his or her own unique style and therefore some may use more leverage than others, and some may not go short at all. All are out to beat the indexes while limiting losses. The right way to look at hedge fund performance is by absolute returns, regardless of market conditions.

Hedge funds continue to thrive because this concept works.

Evidence lies in the number of people and firms that have grown to support hedge funds. Many of these supporting cast members believe that providing goods and services to the industry will be just as profitable as investing in or operating a hedge fund. These people range from consultants and brokers to lawyers and accountants. It is very easy to find a firm that will not only recommend a manager to potential investors but also help a manager find office space, set up phone lines, and install computers. People from all walks of Wall Street have gotten into the hedge fund business, making it relatively easy not only to open a hedge fund but to learn about and invest in one as well.

To understand how hedge funds operate, you need to understand the styles and strategies their managers use. While most conventional money managers own securities in hopes of price appreciation, many hedge fund managers employ alternative strategies that do not rely on the market's going up: short selling, risk *arbitrage*, and the trading of derivatives. Most hedge funds employ strategies that allow them to hedge against risk to ensure that no matter which way the market moves, they are protected against loss.

arbitrage
a financial transaction involving simultaneous purchase in one market and sale in a different market.

There are many benefits to investing in hedge funds. First, I believe that the best and brightest minds in money management have migrated from mutual funds and brokerages to the hedge fund industry. Paying managers for performance ensures that the investor is going to get the fairest shake and that their interest is aligned with the investor's. Add the fact that managers have their own money in the fund and that they can go long and short, and that should be enough for investors to know that their money is in good hands.

As an investor, however, you need to understand what you are getting into and be willing to do research to learn about the manager and the various strategies employed. One of the biggest mistakes people make with any kind of investment is not taking the time to do research. A smart investor is a well-researched investor. If a manager is unwilling to spend time discussing strategy, skills, and background, then investors probably should look elsewhere.

Another mistake is chasing so-called hot money—which is money that flows to the best-performing manager for a quarter or two. The right thing to do is to find managers who perform consistently over time. As an investor you should expect up months and quarters and down months and quarters and, more important, information regarding both periods. It is important to understand where the manager's performance is or is not coming from.

One of the basic tenets of sound investing is portfolio diversification. You should expect managers to explain how they employ it in their portfolios. One of the greatest lessons of the near self-destruction of Long-Term Capital is the need for investors to understand how and where their money is being invested. The idea that a manager wants an investor to have blind faith is ridiculous. Managers should be held accountable and investors should demand to know what is being done with their money.

Despite lapses by some managers and all the media attention, writing this book has made it even more obvious to me that hedge funds are good for investors and managers alike. I believe that by the time you are done reading this book you will believe this as well.

Hedge Fund Basics

For the better part of the past twenty years, the only time the press mentioned hedge funds was when one blew up or some sort of crisis hit one of the world's many markets. All that changed in the late summer of 1998. The currency crisis in Asia spread to Russia, then crept into Europe, and finally hit the shores of the United States in mid-July and early August. Many who follow the markets assumed that things were bad and were going to stay that way for a very long time. And of course the first people who were looked at when the volatility hit was the hedge fund community. Although no one knew for sure what was going on and who and how much was lost, one thing was clear: Many of the most famous hedge funds were in trouble.

After weeks of speculation and rumors, the market finally heard the truth: The world's "greatest investor" and his colleagues had made a mistake. At a little before 4 P.M. eastern standard time (EST) on Wednesday, August 26, Stanley Druckenmiller made the announcement on CNBC in a matter-of-fact way: The Soros organization, in particular its flagship hedge fund, the Quantum Fund, had lost more than $2 billion in recent weeks in the wake of the currency crisis in Russia. The fund had invested heavily in the Russian markets and the trades had gone against them. When the ruble collapsed, the liquidity dried up and there was nothing left to do but hold on to a bunch of worthless slips of paper. During the interview, Druckenmiller did mention that although the fund had sustained significant losses in its Russian investments, overall its total return was still positive for the year, with gains upwards of 19 percent. However, in the months that followed, the Soros organization announced significant changes to the operation including closing one fund that lost over 30 percent.

When asked by the CNBC reporter where the losses came from, Druckenmiller was not specific. It appeared that it was not one trade but a series of trades that had gone against them. The next day, *The New York Times* reported that the fund had also posted losses in dollar bond trades.

When Druckenmiller made the announcement, the Russian equity markets had been down over 80 percent and the government had frozen currency trading as well as stopped paying interest on its debts. The Asian flu had spread, and Russia and many of the other former Soviet republics looked to be in trouble. The difference was that in Russia and the surrounding countries, things looked quite a bit worse than in east Asia.

Although there had been rumors of hedge fund misfortunes and mistakes in these regions, no one knew the true size and scope of the losses. Druckenmiller's announcement was the tip of a very big iceberg and the beginning of a trend in the hedge fund industry, one that was a first: to be open and honest about losses. Hedge fund managers en masse seemed to be stepping up to the plate and admitting publicly that they had made mistakes and had sustained significant losses.

The day after the Soros organization spoke up, a number of other hedge fund managers issued similar statements. Druckenmiller's interview turned out to be the first of several such admissions of losses by famed fund managers. And the losses were staggering.

One fund lost over 85 percent of its assets, going from over $300 million to around $25 million under management. Another said it had lost over $200 million. Others lost between 10 and 20 percent of their assets. They all had come out publicly to lick their wounds, a sort of Wall Street mea culpa.

When the carnage first hit, it seemed that everyone except Julian Robertson, the mastermind behind Tiger Management, the largest hedge fund complex in the world, was the only "name" fund manager not to post losses. Yet even that proved not to be true.

In a statement on September 16, 1998, Robertson said that his funds had lost $2.1 billion or 10 percent of the $20-odd billion he had under management. The losses seemed to come in the early part of September and stemmed from a long-profitable bet on the yen's continuing to fall against the dollar. Because the yen instead appreciated, a number of Robertson's trades declined in value.[1] The funds also saw losses on trades executed in Hong Kong when government authorities intervened in the stock and futures markets to ward off foreign speculators.

Still, like Soros, Tiger was up significantly for the first eight months of 1998. These numbers echoed the funds' performance in recent years with returns in 1996 of over 38 percent and in 1997 of 56 percent. In a letter to investors explaining the losses, Robertson cautioned that the volatility of various markets would make it difficult to continue to post positive returns month after month.

"Sometimes we are going to have a very bad month," he wrote. "We are going to lose money in Russia and in our U.S. longs, and the diversification elsewhere is not going to make up for that, at least not right away. You should be prepared for this."

One of Robertson's investors, who requested anonymity, said that she could not believe all the bad press Robertson received for admitting to the losses. She also questioned whether the reporters really knew what they were talking about when they wrote stories on hedge funds.

"He had some losses, but he is also having a very good year," she said. "The press treats him unfairly because they don't understand what he does or how he does it. They also don't understand how he could be up so much when the mutual funds they themselves are investing in are not performing as well."

However, things were worse at Tiger than the public believed. On November 2, 1998, *The Wall Street Journal* ran a story titled "Robertson's Funds Become Paper Tigers as Blue October Leads to Red Ink for '98." According to the story, the funds had lost over 17 percent or about $3.4 billion through October, which wiped out all of the funds' gains for the year. The funds' total losses through the end of October were approximately $5.5 billion, leaving Tiger with assets of around $17 billion, and it was expected to post losses of 3 percent for the month of November. By the middle of December the funds were down approximately 4 percent for the year.[2] On top of the losses the funds also faced a number of withdrawals from investors both in the United States and abroad. Although a number of industry watchers and observers seemed to believe that Tiger had significant amounts of withdrawals, the firm's public relations firm denied that this was the case. The spokesperson did say that the funds did have "some withdrawals but nothing significant."

Robertson's letter to investors seemed to be the only words of wisdom that investors, traders, and brokers could hold on to as the carnage in the hedge fund industry unfolded. Every day for four or five weeks the financial pages were filled with stories similar to the Robertson and Soros woes.

After all the dust settled and the losses were realized, the hedge fund industry entered its dark period, a direct result of the losses that many big funds posted and the fact that it was the dawn of the technology stock where no investor could do wrong. This period lasted until the tech bubble burst and investors realized that they needed professionals handling their money and that they could not make money on their own. However, in spite of the years that followed the collapse of

Russia, it was clear that Soros and Robertson, both true money masters, and others like them were going to give way to a new breed of managers. The stimulus for this change in the industry was the result of the following incident.

The Near Collapse of Long-Term Capital Management

For most of the summer of 1998, the news about the financial markets was not good. Although many expected to see a recovery in the third and fourth quarter, things took a turn for the worse on September 21, 1998, when the story broke that a large hedge fund was about to collapse and take the markets around the globe with it.

For weeks leading up to that Monday, there had been speculation that Long-Term Capital Management LP (LTCM), a hedge fund with more than $3 billion in assets and run by one of Wall Street's smartest traders, was on the brink of collapse. Earlier in the summer, the firm had announced that it had lost over 44 percent of its assets. Rumors about it not being able to meet *margin calls* were running rampant through Wall Street.

The first real signs that something was dreadfully wrong came when the press broke a story that the New York Stock Exchange had launched an inquiry to determine if the fund was meeting its margin calls from brokers. There had been speculation that some of the brokers were giving Long-Term Capital special treatment and not making it meet its margin obligations, and the NYSE was trying to find out if it was true.

> **margin call**
> demand that an investor deposit enough money or securities to bring a margin account up to the minimum maintenance requirements.

Initially, things at the fund seemed to be under control. It was believed that its managers had put a stop to the hemorrhaging and its operation was returning to normal. These rumors were part truth and part myth. Nobody on Wall Street—not the traders, not the brokers, and least of all the firms that had lent to Long-Term Capital—wanted to believe that it was in dire straits. This was not just some whiz kid trader who had just gotten out of business school and was flying by the seat of his pants. This was John Meriwether, the person who had invented and mastered the use of "rocket science" to make significant returns while limiting risk.

The fund was more than Meriwether; it was managed by some of the smartest minds around Wall Street's trading desks. At the time, Long-Term Capital's partners list read like a who's who of Wall Street's elite. People like Robert Merton and Myron Scholes, both Nobel economics laureates, as well as David Mullins, a former vice chairman of the Federal Reserve Board, were the people making trading decisions and managing its assets. And there were a number of former Salomon Brothers trading whizzes as well as a handful of Ph.D.'s whom Meriwether had groomed personally.

How could this fund blow up? The question seemed ludicrous, especially because the market conditions that existed had often proved to be the ones in which this kind of fund thrived. Wall Street believed that it was impossible for Meriwether to be going the way of Victor Niederhoffer or David Askin—two other high-profile hedge fund managers who lost everything when funds they operated blew up in the mid-1990s.

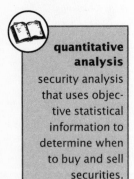

quantitative analysis
security analysis that uses objective statistical information to determine when to buy and sell securities.

Everyone, including himself, believed that Meriwether was the king of quants, as traders who use *quantitative analysis* and mathematics are called, a true master of the universe. People believed that the press had gotten things wrong and that of course the fund would be able to weather the storm.

"He has done it before," they said. "Of course he will do it again." Yet by the end of

September 1998, there was one word to describe the previous statement: *wrong.*

The markets had gotten the best of Meriwether and his partners. He and his team of Ph.D.'s and Nobel laureates had made mistakes that could not be reversed. They had bet the farm and then some and were on the brink of losing it all. The problem was a combination of leverage, risk, and, of course, greed—three ingredients that when mixed together produce one thing: unsustainable losses.

The first news stories came out in late August and early September, after Meriwether announced in a letter to investors that the fund had lost a significant amount of assets. In his letter, which was subsequently published on Bloomberg, Meriwether blamed a number of circumstances for the losses. Still, he said, he and his colleagues and partners believed that the markets would turn in their favor; as long as they continued on the same path, investors would see light at the end of a very dark tunnel.

The letter stated, "Losses of this magnitude are a shock to us as they surely are to you," and that although the firm prided itself on its ability to post returns that are not correlated to the global bond, stock, or currency markets, too much happened too quickly for it to make things right. As with most of Meriwether's communications with investors, the letter did not delve into the types of trades or markets in which the fund was investing. The letter also did not discuss the amounts of leverage Long-Term Capital was using in its drive to capture enormous profits with even the slightest uptick. Nor did it explain that Meriwether had started to trade stock arbitrage positions, something completely different from the bond and currency plays with which he earned his stripes. The letter also failed to mention that the fund had borrowed money from itself to cover its operating expenses.

The simplest explanation of what happened to LTCM is that because multiple markets were hit with multiple crises at the same time—a perfect storm, if you will—there was no way for it to limit its losses or make money. Everything LTCM tried to do failed. Basically, everything that could have gone wrong did. Although the firm specialized in finding unique situations regardless of the condition of the market and employed many "if, then" scenarios, the one thing the partners never were able to figure out was what to do if everything they planned for happened at the same time. The strength of Long-Term Capital's operation rested on the managers' ability to determine what would happen to the prices of many securities when various events hit the market, but their black boxes never told them what would occur if everything they thought possible happened at the same time.

For example, it was widely reported that the fund was short U.S. Treasuries and long high-yield paper and other more risky illiquid investments. The idea was that as Treasury prices fell, yields would increase and the other types of debt instruments would rise in price.

The exact opposite happened. When the turmoil hit the markets, there was an immediate flight to quality, resulting in a significant increase in Treasury prices and a significant decrease in prices of riskier investments. Instead of converging, the trade diverged and ended up going in the wrong direction on both sides of the ticket. When prices of Treasuries shoot up, the yield goes down, and likewise when the prices of high-yield debt go down, the yield increases. Markets that were illiquid to begin with became even more illiquid, and the Treasury market, which has enormous liquidity at all times, showed its lowest yields in a generation.

To understand how the firm could have lost so much so quickly and supposedly even put the world markets at great risk, one first needs to understand how Long-Term Capital operated. The firm specialized in bond arbitrage, a trading strategy Meriwether mastered while working at Salomon Brothers in the 1980s. Traders, using very complex mathematical formulas, capitalize on small price discrepancies among securities in various markets. The idea is to exploit the prices of certain bonds by buying or selling the security based on the perceived value, not the current market value.

The idea behind Long-Term Capital from its outset was to employ this strategy to capture significant profits while enjoying insignificant amounts of risk. Meriwether and his partners were not interested in making a killing on a single trade but rather in picking up small amounts with relatively minor swings in the market from multiple trades. The idea was to employ enough leverage that even the slightest market movement would cause the firm to profit quite handsomely.

If they bought a stock at $100, they would not wait for it to go to $120 or $180 but rather would sell out when it hit $101. Making a dollar does not seem like much, but because their leverage was in excess of 20 to 1 they were able to make big profits on the very small (1 percent) movement. With $100 of equity, the fund would have been able to control $2,000 worth of stock. So in this hypothetical situation, the profit would have been approximately 20 percent. If a $100 investment leveraged at 20 to 1 goes up 10 percent, the trade yields a $200 profit, or a yield of 200 percent on the initial $100, a tripling in value.[3]

In the aftermath of the fund's meltdown, there was of course a lot of Monday morning quarterbacking with very little explanation of what went wrong. *The New York Times* managed to get some unique color on the situation:

> As one Salomon Brothers veteran described it, [Meriwether's] fund was like a roulette player betting on red and doubling up its bets each time the wheel stopped on black. "A gambler with $1,000 will probably lose," he said. "A gambler with $1 billion will wind up owning the casino, because it is a mathematical certainty that red will come up eventually—but you have to have enough chips to stay at the table until that happens."[4]

One thing for sure is that to stay at the table, Meriwether used significant amounts of leverage. The problem was that at Long-Term Capital, leverage got out of hand.

The first indication that things had taken a turn for the worse was in July 1998. Meriwether announced that the fund had posted a loss of some $300 million for the month of June. It was the first time the fund had posted a loss for a month since its inception four years earlier. Reports at the time questioned the veil of secrecy that surrounded the fund's trading and it was unclear where the losses were coming from. The fund had operated in complete silence when it came to discussing strategy or positions, because it believed that once people understood where it was making money, they could determine where its next moves would be and copy its strategies. Very few outside Meriwether's inner circle knew what markets the fund was trading in and where profits and losses originated.

Initial reports had the losses coming from the turmoil that rocked the mortgage-backed securities markets. Still, because of the size of the losses, people suspected that the firm had losses elsewhere, including the currency and U.S. Treasuries markets.

It was quite a shock to many on Wall Street when the losses were announced. For years, Long-Term Capital had performed extremely well and its leader was considered to be too smart to make mistakes. Many others could make mistakes and fail but not John Meriwether and his quants. Wall Street believed that these men and women walked on water. The firm perpetuated the myth time and time again by putting up strong returns, no matter what the condition of the market.

In 1995, the firm was up over 42 percent, net of fees, while in 1996 and 1997 it was up 41 percent and 17 percent respectively. Long-Term Capital did not just beat the indexes; it trounced them.

Still, never would the statement "Past performance is no indication of future results" become more pertinent than during the summer of 1998.

On a very hot day in August, a person I was interviewing for this book told me that Long-Term Capital's losses for June were just the tip of the iceberg; that the firm had sustained enormous losses the previous Friday when buyers dumped corporate bonds and bought Treasuries, sending yields to their lowest point in 20 years. The person told me that a friend had just come from a meeting with a New York investor who said he was pulling out of Long-Term Capital and that Meriwether was on the verge of bankruptcy. I was shocked. On my way out of the interview, I immediately called friends at New York newspapers to try the story. It was possible that other superstars had blown up and of course many smaller hedge funds run by inexperienced managers have failed.

The thought of LTCM failing was ridiculous—it just did not make sense. Its managers were some of the best and brightest on the Street and it just did not seem possible. However, by mid-morning the story had been confirmed; a number of people said that the fund had posted significant losses and looked to be going under.

The next day a number of stories appeared in the papers confirming that Meriwether had lost a significant amount and that the fund needed a large capital infusion to stay afloat. Things looked quite grim for the fund.

It was the first indication that September was going to be a very long month for Long-Term Capital's management and investors, its trading partners, and the entire hedge fund industry.

The story came out because someone leaked a letter that Meriwether had written to investors explaining the situation and requesting new capital. He asked that investors be patient and that they supply him with new capital to "take full advantage of this unusually attractive environment."

People who spoke with him about the letter explained that he believed that by attracting new capital, he would be able to put a hold on the losses and be able to take advantage of the inevitable turnaround that was about to come. However, others believed that it had the making of a Ponzi scheme.

"By continuing to employ strategies that had worked in the past, John believed he would be able to recover from this dreadful situation," a hedge fund manager who is close to Meriwether said. "The problem was people had lost faith. Never had the statement 'you're only as good as your last trade' been more prevalent on Wall Street."

Acknowledgment of the problem came a little too late to stop the hemorrhaging. By the time Meriwether asked for more money, the losses were too great. Even if investors had decided to pony up the extra dollars, they would have only been able to stave off the inevitable for a little while because the need for cash was so great. The well had dried up and the opportunities, it seemed, no longer existed.

At the time he wrote to investors, Meriwether probably did not have any idea where the money to bail out his firm would come from nor the extent of what the bailout would cost. Besides looking for capital from his investors, Meriwether approached outsiders, including Warren Buffett and George Soros, all of whom turned him down.

Buffett did resurface, but as a potential purchaser of the operation, not as an investor. He along with Goldman Sachs Group LP and American International Group Inc. offered to buy the entire operation from Meriwether and to assume the fund's massive portfolios. Meriwether said no, because he did not want to give up control. The press seemed to believe that Meriwether's ego had gotten in the way of getting the deal done with Buffett.

The situation came to a head on Monday, September 21, 1998, when Wall Street's most powerful and influential players got calls from representatives of the Federal Reserve Bank of New York. Some of the recipients were surprised that the Fed was going to intervene in a situation over which it had no direct control.

The president of the New York Fed requested that Wall Street's elite meet to discuss the fate of one of its own. Not since the days of J. P. Morgan had such a group of Wall Street moguls assembled in one room with the intention of devising a plan to save an institution as well as possibly themselves.

Initially, people credited the New York Fed as the stimulus for the bailout, but subsequent reports credited John Corzine, co-managing partner at Goldman Sachs and future senator from New Jersey, as the person who got the ball rolling. Still, it is believed that the Fed prompted him after it started questioning the amount of money Long-Term Capital owed companies under its supervision. It has been suggested that both Goldman Sachs and Merrill Lynch & Co. Inc. had been on the brink of losing so much money because of Long-Term Capital's inability to pay that the Federal Reserve was worried that the firms might themselves be pushed to the brink of insolvency should the fund go bankrupt. Unlike other bankruptcies, when hedge funds go out of business all of their positions are liquidated immediately, in most cases at fire sale prices. It is unknown exactly how much money was at stake, but it is clear that trillions of dollars would have been wiped out if there had been a forced liquidation.

It was also clear that the fund had come to the end of its rope. It needed money to meet its margin obligations or else havoc would reign over the world's already tumultuous markets. For the first time in a very long time the federal government determined that an organization was "too big to fail," and it was going to do everything in its power to ensure that it did not fail. Prior to its involvement in the LTCM bailout the federal government had deemed Chrysler too big to fail and bailed the struggling car maker out in the 1970s with a series of loan guarantees and contracts.

Did the Fed do the right thing? The people I spoke with seemed divided on the issue. Although the debate will go on for some time, one thing is for sure: In light of the takeover by the consortium, Long-Term Capital was able to right itself and started earning money again in the fourth quarter of 1998.

The Federal Reserve had hoped that Goldman Sachs would find a buyer for the fund, but when that failed, it asked the dozen or so companies to come up with a workable solution to this very serious problem.

When the announcement was made that the potential buyer had walked, David Komansky, chairman of Merrill Lynch at the time, took over the discussion to determine to what extent the companies would contribute to keep Long-Term Capital alive and possibly keep a number of themselves from collapsing as well.

After much discussion including some who said they did not want to participate in the bailout but had their minds changed, 14 companies decided to contribute to the bailout, committing sums ranging from $100 million to $350 million. One that did not participate was Bear Stearns & Co., Inc. It was agreed that it should not chip in to the bailout because its risk as Long-Term Capital's clearing broker significantly outweighed the risk posed to other contributors. Table 1.1 illustrates to what extent each company contributed to the bailout.

Although because of the secrecy surrounding the operation it is unclear who lost what, it is apparent that many of Wall Street's

TABLE 1.1　Bailout of Long-Term Capital Management	
$100 Million	*$300 Million*
Banque Parlbas	Bankers Trust
Crédit Agricole	Barclays
Lehman Brothers	Chase Manhattan
	Credit Suisse First Boston
$125 Million	Deutsche Bank
Société Générale	Goldman Sachs
	JP Morgan
	Merrill Lynch
	Morgan Stanley
	Salomon Smith Barney
	Union Bank of Switzerland

Source: The Wall Street Journal, November 16, 1998.

most senior executives took some very big hits when the firm went down. The rescue plan reduced all of the investors' stakes to under 10 percent of what they had been. Executives of some of Wall Street's most prestigious companies—including Merrill Lynch, Bear Stearns, and PaineWebber Group Inc.—faced personal losses. A number of partners at the famed consulting firm McKinsey & Co. lost money as well.

The irony of the situation is that in the wake of the collapse, *The Wall Street Journal, The New York Times,* and *The New York Post* all reported that a number of investors were quite happy that earlier in 1998 Long-Term Capital had returned money to them. Yet most investors who received money back were quite upset at the time. In December 1997, Long-Term Capital had returned approximately $2.7 billion to investors ranging from small money managers to PaineWebber and the Bank of China.

The only firm on Wall Street that seemed to have done well with Long-Term Capital was PaineWebber.[5] It and its chairman and chief executive, Donald Marron, had invested $100 million and $10 million in the fund respectively. Both, however, received money back in 1997. According to a number of reports, the firm more than doubled its investment and Marron got enough money back at least to break even.

Other Wall Streeters were not so lucky. Bear Stearns chief executive James Cayne and executive vice president Warren Spector are believed to have lost more than $9 million each. Merrill Lynch's Komansky, who along with over a hundred of his colleagues had invested approximately $22 million in the fund, saw that position reduced to less than $2 million once the bailout was complete.

The idea that a hedge fund got too big to fail is quite remarkable. By the time the bailout agreement was reached, Long-Term Capital had received commitments in excess of $3.5 billion to be used to meet margin calls and to cover operating expenses. The bailout was designed to ensure that the firm would not collapse and cause credit markets around the world to cave in from dumping its positions. It is believed that if the fund had been forced to liquidate, it might have caused the undermining of more than $1 trillion in assets. However, this is pure speculation and we will never really know what could have happened had the fund truly gone down.

This experience makes it quite clear that the bull market of the mid- and late 1990s had gotten out of control and once again an enormous level of greed had come over the Street. The only way Long-Term Capital was able to become so large was that it was lent money without any regard for whether it could pay back what it borrowed. The lenders looked instead to the fees associated with the transactions and the continuous stream of revenue the firm would provide to line the brokerages' and banks' pockets.

In the wake of the Long-Term Capital disaster, the calls for hedge fund reform and regulation swept the nation and the world. Congress held hearings and industry observers cried foul, but hedge funds took a backseat to the scandal and impeachment that rocked the White House. Nothing came of the hearings and no new regulations were put in place.

The New York Times reported that one Wall Street executive who was briefed on the negotiations that led to the bailout said that he had learned a lesson about his own firm's operation after reviewing its exposure to Long-Term Capital.

"We will never let our exposure to one counterparty get to these levels again—never. He had gotten too big for the market," he said of Meriwether. "Everybody gave him too much money."[6]

A few months later after the bailout, however, things had started to turn around for Long-Term Capital Management and Meriwether. First the hedge fund reported profits and then came the speculation the fund was looking to buy out its saviors and that if an amicable arrangement could not be met, Meriwether would start a new investment vehicle. While the buyout never seemed to materialize, the fund's financial situation had completely turned around by the spring of 1999. Meriwether and his partners had paid back a significant portion of the bailout and had started talking about a new fund that they planned on launching.

In the early fall, Long-Term Capital had paid back close to 75 percent of the bailout to the consortium of financial institutions that had saved it a year earlier. The consortium issued a statement at the end of September stating that "the portfolio is in excellent shape" and that risk profile of the fund had been reduced by nearly 90 percent. One of the stipulations of the bailout was that before the Long-Term Capital's managers could operate a new fund, they had to repay 90 percent of the money the banks put into it. This meant that the fund needed to repay an additional $600 million to the consortium before Meriwether and his partners could raise money for a new fund.

By December 1999, LTCM fully repaid the banks that had prevented its collapse. Weeks later, the fund was quietly closed. Some investors are still sitting on losses. Meriwether has since gone on to launch a new hedge fund that employs similar investment strategies as LTCM called JWM Partners LLC.

A Brief History of Hedge Funds

It used to be that if you queried students at business schools about where they wanted to work after graduation, responses would be names like Salomon Brothers, Goldman Sachs, or Morgan Stanley as well as General Motors, Coca-Cola, or IBM.

Now, however, students say they want to work for firms like SAC Capital, Maverick Capital, and The Clinton Group—in other words, hedge funds, organizations that were not on the radar screen of Middle America until the near collapse of Long-Term Capital. Still, on Wall Street these firms have always been looked at with awe.

Once considered a small and obscure pocket of the Street, these firms represent one of the fastest-growing areas of the financial world.

Because of their nature, hedge funds are supposed to thrive regardless of market conditions.

To understand how the hedge fund industry evolved, one needs first to understand where the concept came from. Let's define what a hedge fund is and how it works.

The term was coined by Alfred Winslow Jones, a sociologist, author, and financial journalist who got interested in the markets while writing about Wall Street for *Fortune* magazine in the 1940s.

Jones started the first known hedge fund in 1949 and as such defined the term by his style of investing, management, and organizational structure.

Although Jones is credited with laying the foundation for the industry, many on Wall Street believe Roy Neuberger, the founder of the securities firm Neuberger Berman, Inc., was the person who created the concept of a hedge fund. Others believe it was Benjamin Graham, the father of securities analysis, who devised the method and formula for paying managers.

Regardless, when people think of the history of hedge funds and where they came from, they always think of Alfred Winslow Jones.

The problem is that many do not know about the Jones organization or his investment style or how he defined his hedge fund. In fact, there had not been an article of substance written about Jones for more than 20 years until October 1998, when *Grant's Interest Rate Observer* published a significant story on Jones in the wake of the near collapse of Long-Term Capital.

The industry has changed quite substantially since Jones launched his fund, A. W. Jones & Co. The most important change is to the definition of what he created.

Today the popular press defines hedge funds as private investment pools of money that wealthy individuals, families, and institutions invest in to protect assets and to achieve rates of return above and in fact well beyond those offered by mutual funds or other investment opportunities. For the most part, the press is correct. Where it errs is in defining the methodology as well as the concept of these private investment vehicles for sophisticated investors.

More importantly, in light of recent industry changes and pending regulations, the hedge fund industry is going to be open to more and more investors. Investors with as little as $50,000 can now access hedge funds and the minimum investment is going lower and lower. By the end of 2005 and early 2006, investors with as little as $10,000 will be able to own hedge funds. The industry is becoming more and more mainstream as a direct result of traditional long-only managers' inability to put up consistent returns over a long period of time. Today retail investors have realized that they need to be both long and short the market just as Jones did 50-odd years ago.

We'll discuss later the intricacies of how hedge funds operate as well as just who invests in them and why. The term "hedge fund" is like most things on Wall Street—it sounds tricky but once it is dissected it is quite easy to understand.

It is my belief from talking to colleagues, relatives, and friends of Jones that he had no intention of creating a difficult product. Rather, I believe he would have wanted the masses to understand his idea of the use of hedges to minimize risk and hoped that it would be employed more widely throughout the investing world.

One of the reasons hedge funds were obscure until the Long-Term Capital debacle is the way the press describes their trading operations and styles. Reporters seem to be afraid of scratching more than the surface, but truly enjoy using the term for shock purposes in news stories with headlines like "Soros Loses $2 Billion in Russia" or "Robertson's Tiger Pounces."

These are simple words that grab attention with little or no explanation of the operation. It is not all the fault of the press in most cases, since hedge fund managers hide behind Securities and Exchange Commission rules regarding marketing and solicitation. The

SEC does not allow managers to market their funds or to solicit investors that are not prequalified, and talking to the press could be construed as marketing. Still, the information usually gets out and I believe it would do the industry good if managers were a little less tight-lipped.

For the most part, everyone I asked to talk about their own business and the industry spoke freely and I believe honestly. Also, in the past few years or so, in light of a number of financial crises, it seems managers are opening up more. This, in my opinion, can only help the industry.

Since Jones created the hedge fund industry, only three articles have been written about him that have any real merit or worth. Two are by the same journalist and ran in *Fortune* magazine, while the third was published in *Institutional Investor*.

To understand how important the articles are to the industry, we first need to understand the Jones model. No matter how far managers today deviate from the definition, each and every one operates with some of Jones's original characteristics.

According to Jones, as described by Carol Loomis in her January 1970 article in *Fortune* titled "Hard Times Come to the Hedge Funds" (still considered to be one of the definitive articles on Jones and the industry), a hedge fund is a *limited liability company* structured so as to give the general partners—the managers— a share of the profits earned on the investor's money. Further, a hedge fund always uses leverage and always carries some short positions. Jones called his investment vehicle a "hedged fund"—a fund that is hedged and is protected against market swings by the structure of its long and short positions. Somewhere along the line Wall Street's powers that be dropped the "d."

limited liability company
a legal structure that is the hedge fund investment vehicle.

The method for sharing in the profits is defined in the hedge fund's fee structure. Under the Jones scenario, the managers receive 20 percent of the portfolio's profits—and nothing else. Therefore they have quite an incentive to pick winners and, more importantly, to do right by the investors.

In recent years, managers have added a *management fee* of 1 to 1.5 percent of assets to the 20 percent *performance fee*. It is unclear who decided to add this fee, but like most things on Wall Street, when it works people copy it. This fee basically allows the managers to cover the cost of maintaining the fund's operations as well as providing a bit of a salary. The Jones organization never levied management fees on its partners.

> **management fee**
> fee paid to the manager for day-to-day operation of the hedge fund.

According to Robert Burch, Jones's son-in-law and the current operator of A. W. Jones & Co., Jones never believed in management fees.

"He believed that [management fees] would only breed more assets and take away from the concept of performance and induce

> **performance fee**
> fee paid to manager based on how well the investment strategy performs.

the fact that you could make more money building assets than through performing according to the model," says Burch. "Jones was concerned with performance and did not want to be distracted by asset-gathering."

For the most part, the Jones model worked well in both up and down markets, as it was intended to do. In its first 20 years of operation, the system worked so well that the Jones fund never had a losing year. It was not until the bear market of the late 1960s and 1970 that it posted losses.

The hedge fund industry has truly grown very large very fast. It seems that everyone who wants to be in the money management business wants to work for or own a hedge fund. This is not theory but practice, as many mutual fund managers, traders, and analysts are jumping ship to start their own funds. These people are setting up entities that they call a hedge fund and—voilà!—they are in the business.

The problem is that many who are calling themselves hedge fund managers are not. To have a hedge fund you have to *hedge*. Therefore, those who do not hedge but call themselves a hedge fund are operating nothing more than a very expensive mutual fund.

Many managers still follow the classical Jones model, using leverage and having long and short positions that allow you to maximize returns while limiting risks in both rising and falling markets. Probably the person who best exemplifies the Jones model today is Julian Robertson.

Robertson, who is discussed in Chapter 2, is considered by most to be the person who took over Jones's spot as the dean of the hedge fund industry. Although his fund organization is no longer in existence, Robertson best exemplifies what Jones had in mind when he defined and developed his idea.

Robertson, who covered Jones while he worked at Kidder Peabody, built an enormously successful business, at one time managing in excess of $20 billion. Like most other hedge fund managers, Robertson lost a considerable amount of money in the turmoil of 1998—more than 10 percent of his assets under management, and in the wake of the euphoria surrounding technology stocks opted to shut his funds down and return assets to investors rather than invest in stocks of companies that he did not understand. Today Robertson operates a hedge fund incubator of sorts, working with new managers to help them build their businesses while actively trading the markets with his own capital. Robertson's legacy is that his organization bred success and many of the people who passed through Tiger's doors have gone on to do great things in the hedge fund industry. It is estimated that nearly 20 percent of all of the assets allocated to hedge funds is run by someone who formerly worked at Tiger—one of the so-called Tiger Cubs. Although Robertson is known to be an arrogant, egomaniacal hard worker, he is possibly the greatest money manager of all time.

"Julian is the natural successor to Jones," says Burch. "He has built a business around the principles and disciplines that Jones used to build his business. He understands the Jones model and uses it to make superior returns regardless of market conditions."

The Current State of the Hedge Fund Industry

It is impossible to get an absolute number of how many hedge funds exist or the exact amount of assets the industry as a whole has under management. The numbers of both change as fast as you can make telephone calls to people who track this information. The SEC requires mutual funds and corporations to report financial information to it quarterly, which makes these data literally just a click away.

With hedge funds it is not so easy. There is no regulation or requirement for fund managers to report data. Many fund managers are quite happy reporting data when profits are up; but as soon as things go south, the information does not flow so freely. Often, a fund manager also ignores the tracking companies when the fund reaches investor capacity and can no longer accept investment dollars from outside its current group of investors. In this case, the fund manager no longer needs the tracking service, because new investors will only have to be turned away.

For the purposes of this book, I am going to define the size and scope of the industry as follows: There are 8,000 hedge funds with $850 billion under management.

In 1971, an SEC report on institutional investors estimated that hedge funds had $1.06 billion under management.[7] At the time, the

SEC found that Alfred Winslow Jones's organization had just under 23 percent of all of the assets under management placed with hedge funds.[8]

Today, a hedge fund can be any sort of private investment vehicle that is created as either a limited partnership or a limited liability corporation. In either case, the vehicle falls under very narrow SEC and Internal Revenue Service (IRS) rules and regulations. It is limited as to how many investors it can have, either 100 or 500 depending on its structure. The structure also determines the type of investors it can accept, either accredited or superaccredited.[9] Institutions that include nonfinancial companies are able to invest in either type of fund.

In light of the hedge fund debacle of 1998, Congress and other U.S. officials have been pressing for more controls and monitoring systems for the industry. In the fall of 2004, the SEC voted to require all hedge fund managers with 15 or more investors and $25 million or more in assets under management to register as a Registered Investment Advisor. The ruling was adopted by the SEC and put in place effective February 1, 2006. Once registered the fund manager would come under the authority of the SEC similar to the way mutual funds are regulated by the commission. It is questionable what, if any, impact this new regulation will have on the industry and its participants.

The reason many of Wall Street's traders and would-be traders are flocking to set up and work for hedge funds is because the industry is considered by some to be the last bastion of capitalism.

"When we started, it was very difficult to get through the paperwork and raise capital," says Jim Rogers, who was George Soros's partner for more than 10 years. "Now it is very easy and people specialize in setting up the funds and raising capital. It is probably the most efficient way to make money in the financial world."

Rogers's sentiments are echoed in an article about hedge funds that appeared in the popular press. The articles describe a number of start-up funds and their managers. Why do they leave their soft jobs at white-shoe investment firms to go out on their own? The answers: freedom and money.

According to one article, written by Bethany McLean of *Fortune* magazine, "No other career in finance gives you the freedom to be your own boss and invest in anything, anywhere, that gets your juices flowing," or provides these people with the opportunity to "get so rich, so fast, so young."[10]

McLean quoted one manager's quip: "I can wager your money on the Knicks game if I want."[11] This is true, it is legal, and it is very, very scary.

A number of former Jones employees have said that many of these people would not have been able to work for their company nor to succeed in the markets in which the Jones organization thrived. Clearly statements like the one above were not what Jones had in mind when he developed hedge funds.

Still, to understand this and where the idea of a hedge fund came from as well as how the business was born, one needs to learn about the father of it all.

Alfred Winslow Jones— The Original Hedge Fund Manager

Alfred Winslow Jones started what has come to be known as the first hedge fund in 1949. His basic investment strategy was to use leverage in combination with long and short sales in order to hedge risk should the market turn against him.

Jones, who died at the age of 88 in June of 1989, devised a formula for the vehicle while researching a freelance article for *Fortune* titled "Fashion in Forecasting," which ran in the March 1949 issue. To research the piece, he spent many hours speaking with some of Wall Street's great traders and brokers. Upon learning their methods, he devised his own ideas on investing based around the concept of hedging—something very few people did in those days. And so with three partners he launched the fund at the age of 49.

"My father took a very long time to find himself," says Anthony Jones, one of Jones's two children. "He graduated from college with some of the same loose ends that many people who graduate have today and basically tried a number of things before he realized what he wanted to do."

After traveling the world on a tramp steamer as purser, he believed he had found himself when he joined the Foreign Service.

"He was in Germany in the early thirties and watched the rise of Hitler and then was assigned to Venezuela, and the prospect of going from Berlin to Venezuela was so depressing that he quit the Foreign Service," Tony Jones says. "He came to the United States and got involved in sociology."

Jones's interests in sociology and the idea of how social movements developed led him to enter Columbia University. He earned a Ph.D. in sociology in 1941, and it was at Columbia where he met Benjamin Graham.

"His graduate work was interrupted by my parents' marriage and their honeymoon took them to civil war Spain," says Tony Jones. "In Spain they did a survey for the Quakers—neither of them carried a rifle or drove an ambulance—and toured around with interesting people reporting on civilian relief."

Upon returning to the United States, Jones took a job with *Fortune,* where he worked until 1946. Whether he knew it or not, it was here where he would be laying the groundwork for a lifetime career.

After leaving *Fortune,* he worked as a freelancer for it and other magazines, writing on social and political issues as well as finance. The research and reporting Jones did for "Fashion in Forecasting" convinced him that working on Wall Street was not as difficult as many believed.

"He would come home every day while he was reporting the piece and tell me that he did not learn anything new," recalled his widow, Mary. "After a while he started working on an idea and finally came up with something he believed would work." Mary Jones died on January 8, 1999, at the age of 91.

The article looked at how stock market behavior was interpreted by technicians of statistics, charts, and trends. The following is an excerpt of the piece.

> The standard, old-fashioned method of predicting the course of the stock market is first to look at facts and figures external to the market itself, and then examine stock prices to see whether they are too high or too low. Freight-car loadings, commodity prices, bank clearings, the outlook for tax legislation, political prospects, the danger of war, and countless other factors determine corporations' earnings and dividends, and these, combined with money rates, are supposed to (and in the long run do) determine the prices of common stocks. But in the meantime awkward things get in the way (and in the long run, as Keynes said, we shall be dead).
>
> In the late summer of 1946, for instance, the Dow Jones industrial stock average dropped in five weeks from 205 to 163, part of the move to a minor panic. In spite of the stock market, business was good before the break, remained good through it, and has been good ever since.
>
> Nevertheless there are market analysts, whose concern is the internal character of the market, who could see the decline coming. To get these predictive powers they study the statistics that the stock market itself grinds out day after day. Refined, manipulated in various ways, and interpreted, these data are sold by probably as many as twenty stock-market services and are used independently by hundreds, perhaps thousands, of individuals. They are increasingly used by brokerage firms, by some because the users believe in them and by others because their use brings in business.[12]

"I was a young kid at the time the business was started, and I have no recollection of when he stopped going to work at *Fortune* or writing and started going to work for himself," says Tony Jones. "I do have quite fond memories of going to visit him at his office down at 80 Broad Street in the heart of Wall Street."

Jones's model for his fund had a very simple formula. He basically used leverage and short sales to create a system that allowed him to concentrate on stock picking rather than market timing.

According to Tony Jones, he realized very early on that he was not a good stock picker. Indeed, Tony Jones believes that it was this realization that led him to expand the organization, bringing in budding Wall Street stars to run the partnership's money, to the point where it became successful.

"He was a good salesman; he knew people to raise money from, and was a good organizer and administrator. But when it came to picking stocks, he had no particular talent," he says. "This meant that his job was to find people who did have talent."

Working for and with the Jones organization was very lucrative. All partners received a piece of the 20 percent that Jones was paid by the limited partners and they were able to invest in the vehicle.

Brokers knew that if they had an idea and the Jones people liked it, they could sell it over the phone. One broker told me that he used to like to run all of his ideas by the Jones people before calling other clients. He knew that they would act immediately if they liked his idea, but also would tell him if the situation would not work and in turn helped him from pushing a bad stock.

"These were some of the smartest and savviest investors and traders of the time," the broker says. "They gave you a straight scoop on the situation. It was a lot of fun covering the account."

Besides developing the hedge fund, the Jones organization perfected the art of paying brokers to give up ideas. Although the firm executed most of its orders through Neuberger Berman, Inc., it paid brokers for ideas. Should a broker call on one of Jones's managers, he knew that if the manager used his idea, he would be paid regardless of where the order was executed.

"When Jones's people got an idea, they would call us and execute the order and tell us where the idea came from," remembers Roy Neuberger. "We would give up half of the commission to the guy who came up with the idea, whether he worked for us or not. At the time I did not think the exchange would let us do it. But they did, no ifs, ands, or buts; it was perfectly all right with them."

Neuberger continues, "For many years, the Jones account was the firm's most important account. But it was more than business. We were friends; both he and his wife were friends of my wife and me, and we socialized together."

Jones's strength seemed to be in people as well as ideas. His organization gave birth to many successful managers.

"There were a whole bunch of people who used to work for my father that went on their own," recalls Tony Jones. "After a while he began a business of farming the money out and created a sort of hedge fund of hedge funds."

"Jones made no attempt to pick stocks; he was an executive," says Neuberger. "He understood how to get things done and how to find people to execute his ideas."

One former Jones employee told me that the hardest part of working for Jones was actually getting the invitation to work for him. Jones used a number of techniques to tell the good from the bad, one of which was a paper portfolio program.

"In order to work for my father you first had to prove yourself," Tony Jones says. "To prove yourself, you needed to manage a play portfolio of stocks over a period of, say, six months or so. Every day, you had to call in your trades to the firm and they would be 'executed.' It was only after my father was able to watch how the manager was doing with the play money that he invited them in as partners."

The firm tallied up the profits and losses and examined not only how well the prospective managers performed but also how they did it.

"When it came to hiring managers, my father was very cautious," Tony Jones says. "He wanted to know how they operated and watched very carefully to see what types of decisions they made with the play money. If everything worked out, they got a job."

Another interesting point of the Jones organization was that he did not fire people. If you performed poorly, he simply did not give you any more money to manage and took pieces away little by little so eventually there was nothing left. And the manager had to leave.

From all accounts, Jones was very satisfied and proud of his invention and he appreciated the publicity that he received. Yet he was not very interested in talking about money or the stock market.

"Jones was not a man who was very interested in Wall Street or making money; rather he was interested in the intellectual challenge of it all," says son-in-law Burch. "Although he made a lot of money, he was not very interested in spending and gave a lot of his money away, creating things like the Reverse Peace Corps and other foundations to help people here in the United States."

Jones was very involved with a number of charitable organizations in New York City. One cause to which he was a major contributor and in which his son and daughter are still quite active is the Henry Street Settlement.

Founded in 1893 by Lillian Wald on Manhattan's Lower East Side, the Henry Street Settlement provides programs that range from transitional residences for homeless families and a mental health clinic to a senior services center and a community arts center.

"My father liked to travel to Third World countries. He liked to have a mission, but he had a notion that a number of nations criticized the United States for not doing enough to help out on their own shores and that drew him to Henry Street," remembers Dale Burch, Jones's daughter. "He liked the fact that it helped the community from within itself."

Jones also created an operation called Globalization for Youth, an antipoverty program that used a number of resources to keep children from getting into trouble.

"These are the types of things we talked about," says Tony Jones. "He was very concerned with family solidarity and all of the theories that evolved in the late fifties and early sixties that are currently social work orthodoxy."

Once he launched his fund, he very rarely talked about what he did or how he did it. "When you had dinner with Jones, you always had four or five guys from various parts of the world," recalls Burch. "You didn't know if that night you were going to discuss some pending revolt in Albania or what language they were speaking in Iran.

"It was an interesting challenge to participate in the dinner conversation. The discussion was never about money and never about Wall Street—his mind was way beyond that," he continues.

Tony Jones recalls that when the family went to their country home in Connecticut, his mother would drive and his father would go through the evening newspaper with a list of all the stocks his managers had and calculate how they had done that day.

That was the extent to which he brought the business home.

"There was absolutely no time for discussions of what stocks might go up or down at home," says Tony Jones.

Jones did not have many of the characteristics of other Wall Street legends. For example, according to his son, at Christmastime when the brokerages his firm did business with wanted to give him presents, he would accept only items that could be consumed.

"Many of the Wall Street firms tried desperately to give him gifts as a thank-you for all of the revenue he generated, and he would never accept anything except for something he could eat in the next week," Tony Jones recollects. "We got a Christmas turkey from Neuberger Berman but when it came to gold cuff links or the like, forget about it."

Roy Neuberger called Jones a thinker, not necessarily a hard worker, a sentiment that seems to be echoed by his son.

"My father's entire life was preoccupied with ideas, some crazy and some not so crazy," Tony Jones says. "He had the capacity to read a book and then just get on the phone and call the author up and have lunch. He got to know people and many things and was constantly thinking about everything under the sun."

According to Tony Jones, after his father read a book claiming that the works of Shakespeare had been written by the 16th Earl of Oxford, he decided that the theory was sound and talked about it for two years.

"After his journalism days, and getting in the business, he did not really have long-term interests," Tony Jones says. "He was more interested in things he could focus on short-term. The idea of tackling big projects was not something he was interested in."

Besides countless articles, Jones did publish one book, *Life, Liberty, and Property,* in 1941, based on his doctoral dissertation. According to Daniel Nelson, a history professor at the University of Akron, it was the rarest of dissertations: technically sophisticated, engaging, and addressed to a general audience. A new edition of the book was published in March 1999 by the University of Akron Press.

Although most of the articles written about Jones say he had planned to write a second book, his son says he wanted to but "it would have been a monumental task." When Jones retired from the hedge fund business completely in 1982, he was satisfied with the business but not with its being his life's work.

"Later on in his life, he wanted to write a memoir but could not focus himself on getting it done," Tony Jones says. "There was nothing about running his business that required real concentration—it was a brainstorm kind of thing and he was good at it."

Jones did not simply hit an age and retire. Rather, he started to give up his duties at the firm and eventually turned the reins over to Lester Kissel. Kissel, a lawyer from the firm Seward & Kissel and an original partner in A. W. Jones & Co., assumed control for a few years. Because of conflicts over the direction of the organization, he was asked to step down and after a brief stint by Jones, Burch took over. Today Burch and his son run A. W. Jones in New York City as a fund of funds.

"My father was not at the top of his game when he turned things over to Kissel," says Tony Jones. "Kissel was a lawyer, not a businessman. He never did anything intentionally to harm my father but he did hurt the business."

By today's standards, Jones did not become extraordinarily wealthy from the business. Still, he spent the bulk of the money he did have on charities, not on lavish living.

However, one of Jones's great loves was his 200-acre estate in Connecticut that allowed him to enjoy the outdoors.

"My father was a landscape visionary," says his son. "He was always trying to figure out things to do with water and moving land around.

"His mind was all over the place," he continues. "Everything he did, did not require an enormous amount of steady follow-through on his part. He had a lot of good ideas and made them reality."

Tony Jones believes his father's reason for switching from journalism to Wall Street was that he wanted to live comfortably and he knew that he could not achieve that as a journalist.

"He had carved out a unique niche for himself writing but realized that he would never be able to live the kind of lifestyle he wanted to being a journalist," says Tony Jones. "My father was also determined to find out if his crazy idea would work."

Although most people point to the research for the *Fortune* article as the genesis, a number I talked to seem to think a combination of things led him to the hedge fund concept.

It is quite clear that while Jones was studying at Columbia he had many conversations with Graham and learned investing strategies from him. This may be where the seeds of the idea were planted.

Jones did know another Graham follower, Warren Buffett, and the two lunched together from time to time.

"The principles of the hedge fund were clearly developed and created by Alfred. However, some of his investment strategies may have come from his discussions with Buffett and Graham," says Burch. "He was the first to put the ideas down on paper and then actually put them to use."

Jones defined the principles of hedge funds as follows:

1. You had to be short all the time.

2. You always use leverage.

3. The manager receives a fee of 20 percent of all profits.

"It was the combinations of shorting, the use of leverage, and the fee structure, which is how Jones defined what a hedge fund was all about," says Burch.

Jones believed that by aggressively picking long stocks and neutralizing market swings by also being short, he would be able to put up extraordinary performance numbers while reducing risks.

At all times, Jones's funds maintained a number of short positions that would enable them to have a hedge against a drop in the market, which limited his downside exposure. It is impossible to get a complete accounting of the fund's track record because of the private nature of its activities and investors.

According to Jones's *New York Times* obituary, in the 10 years prior to 1968 the firm had posted gains up to 1,000 percent. It is estimated that the Jones fund had over $200 million under management at the end of that period.

Soon after that, however, things began to not go very well and the Jones organization, like many other hedge funds, took a serious hit. By year-end 1970, the Securities and Exchange Commission estimated that the fund organization had a mere $30 million under management. It is unclear exactly where the money went, but some was lost to market mistakes and the rest vanished as partners pulled out.

Interestingly enough, the only fund the SEC tracked during that same time period that did not see a decrease in assets was Steinhardt Fine Berkowitz & Co., headed by the soon-to-be-legendary Michael Steinhardt.

By 1977, when the hedge fund industry had plummeted from over $2 billion to roughly $250 million under management, many in the industry thought the concept had seen its day.

Jones himself was quoted in an article in *Institutional Investor* in May 1977 as saying, "I don't believe it [a hedge fund] is ever going to become a big part of the investment scene as it was in the 1960s. . . . The hedge fund does not have a terrific future."[13]

Indeed, as with all things associated with the markets, hedge funds had been going through a rough time; but the cycle soon righted itself. Slowly but surely, through the late 1970s and the 1980s, the industry got back on its feet. It was the bull market of the 1990s, however, that really put hedge funds on the map.

Today the combination of shorting and going long in stocks is second nature to even the most immature Wall Streeter, but 30 years ago it was a daring concept.

Loomis, in her piece "Hard Times Come to the Hedge Funds," wrote that her previous story on hedge funds, "The Jones Nobody Keeps Up With," inspired some people to start their own funds, using "the article about Jones as a sort of prospectus, relying on it for help in explaining, and selling, the hedge fund concept to investors."[14]

Slowly but surely, Jones is continuing to get the recognition he deserves. Whether people realize it or not, and I think most do, Alfred Winslow Jones, the sociologist and businessman, created one of Wall Street's most important concepts. His invention gave life to thousands of entrepreneurs and has made and will continue to make many people very wealthy for years to come.

2

How Hedge Funds Operate

This chapter explores how hedge funds operate and why blaming them for the ills that rock Wall Street is silly. It is important to understand how to start a hedge fund, who is investing in the vehicles, and who provides services to the industry. It is here that you will read about "the world's greatest investor" and how he came to get this title.

The sport of blaming hedge funds for financial meltdowns was never more apparent than in the summer of 1998 when volatility rocked the world's markets. The near collapse of Long-Term Capital Management LP was splashed across newspapers around the globe, as both a victim and cause of its own demise. Reporters and editors had found a scapegoat for any financial disasters that occurred. However, since then, hedge funds have lost their role as a scapegoat for all that is wrong with the market, partly because we have not had many serious financial scandals and partly because hedge funds have become more mainstream.

It's easy, and it does make a lot of sense, to blame the hedge funds. First, most of them shun publicity and refuse to speak on the record about their strategies or investments. Second, many organizations, including the International Monetary Fund (IMF) and the World Bank, not to mention the Securities and Exchange Commission (SEC) and the Federal Reserve System, have trouble tracking hedge fund operators' moves.

So why shouldn't society blame such secretive organizations for its financial woes? When problems strike, why not blame those who are doing well, because surely their success comes at the expense of others?

To understand why blaming hedge funds for every currency crisis and Dow drop is downright silly, we first need to look at who is operating and investing in them. Many of the hedge funds that were once blamed for wreaking havoc on the world's markets were in a state of turmoil as the Asian and Russian crisis of the summer of 1998 took hold. One fund manager believed that Long-Term Capital Management's woes were just the tip of the iceberg and that by year's end more than half of the funds in existence would no longer be around.

"People are not interested in losing money," he said. "The whole reason why investors go with hedge funds is because they want superior returns but also want to be protected when the markets get shaky. Losing half of your assets is not the type of protection that most people have in mind."

This thankfully did not come true. And while many funds did fall, the market events are cyclical. The late summer of 1998, the tech bubble of 2000, and the bear market of 2002 displayed a lot of the same characteristics of the 1970s and early 1980s when hedge funds hit hard times. Earlier, the funds had been on a tear, posting very strong returns and attracting many investors and imitators.

For most of the 1950s and 1960s, many people copied and tried to imitate Jones and his staff's method of investing and trading. They wanted to emulate the Jones model, which used a series of long and

short positions to put up very significant returns. This strategy worked until the *bear market* started in 1969, when these investment
partnerships took it on the chin; most of them
eventually went out of business.

bear market
prolonged period of falling prices.

The *Fortune* magazine piece titled "Hard Times Come to the
Hedge Funds" written by Carol Loomis in January 1970 captures the
essence of the hedge fund phenomenon and its explosion. At the
time, Loomis estimated that 150 funds around the country had assets
under management totaling $1 billion. The hook of the story was that
many of the fund managers had not seen 1969's bear market coming.
In fact, some funds, including A. W. Jones's, had been negative or flat
for the year, causing many of the fund managers to change their
strategies and reevaluate their business models. A few went out of
business altogether.

Jones's two partnerships each finished 1969 down over 30 percent for the year, while the New York Stock Exchange composite was
off 13 percent.

One of the most interesting points of Loomis's article is revealed in
Jones's comments that the problems of 1969 were predicated on Wall
Street's "craze for performance" and that "money managers . . . got over-
confident about their ability to make money."[1]

One needs only to look at other recent articles in the mainstream
press about hedge funds to see that the same sort of euphoria is sweep-
ing the industry today. In the past 10 years, their numbers have exploded. Since 1990, the assets that hedge funds manage have grown
tenfold while the number of hedge funds has ballooned at approximately the same rate.

Some people estimate that a new hedge
fund opens every day and believe that until the
bull market bubble truly bursts and enough
people get badly hurt, there will be no end to
this trend. One person close to the industry told

bull market
prolonged period of rising prices.

me that the best thing to happen to hedge funds is that Wall Street is having problems.

"As long as firms continue to lay off people and pay significantly smaller bonuses, the [hedge fund] industry will continue to be strong," he said. "If you lose your job, what could be easier than setting up a fund? And if you get a small bonus, you think that you can do it yourself and don't need anyone."

As history tells us time and again, the market is about cycles. Hedge funds are not going to be wiped out completely, but it is inevitable that once the bull leaves the ring, a number of them will vanish and the explosive growth in the industry will subside. If some of the biggest, smartest, and most powerful funds took such huge hits from technology, Russia, and Asia, prudent thinkers have to believe that others will go down as well.

"It is very simple. A lot of people follow the herd mentality. Right now the herd is going into hedge funds," says one hedge fund manager who requested anonymity. "Eventually, the herd gets wiped out."

Starting a Hedge Fund

Today pretty much anyone with a few dollars can start a hedge fund. The most important character traits needed are an ego, an entrepreneurial spirit, and guts. A track record also helps, but in some cases experience is frowned upon—although it is very difficult for a manager to raise significant assets without some sort of track record. In most cases, institutional investors—pension plans, endowments and insurance companies—like to see at least three years of performance before they invest. However, individual investors do not seem to be so picky and will invest with new managers with little or no track record.

A budding manager needs somewhere between $25,000 and $50,000 to cover the costs of the legal work as well as some initial capital. Some managers start with as little investment capital as $25,000, while others jump out of the gate with millions or even billions. Once the entity is created and a brokerage account is opened, the manager is in business.

The advances in technology in the past few years have made gathering investment ideas as easy as picking up the phone. Many would-be A. W. Joneses are setting up shop in their living rooms, installing computers and phone lines and placing trades.

One manager told me that it is much more efficient to trade out of his apartment on Manhattan's Upper West Side than from an office downtown. He doesn't have to waste time commuting and he can work no matter what time of day it is without the hassle of riding the subway.

"I no longer need to be on the ground in every country I want to invest in, nor do I have to worry about reporting accounting or brokerage functions because of the strides made in technology in the last few years," says the manager. "Most of the initial information I need is available on the Bloomberg or the Web, and by having a personal computer hooked into both, the information is literally a click away. Technology allows me to get the process started a lot quicker and makes the investment process a lot more manageable. It allows me to kick the tires of more companies faster than ever before." "Kicking the tires" is a theme that many of today's up-and-coming managers employ when they go after investment ideas.

It used to be that if you wanted information on companies in Senegal or on stocks in Australia, you needed to be on the ground in the country or wait until your broker opened an office there. Today, the speed at which information travels provides managers access to news and research 24 hours a day, seven days a week. You now can not only get a quote on any stock anywhere in the world but you can also get a map on how to get there by pointing your Web browser to a site and clicking the mouse.

Paul Wong, the former manager of Edgehill Capital, constructed what he called "Hedge Fund Heaven," an office off the entryway of his home in Connecticut where he managed his portfolio and handled all fund operations. In his slice of heaven, Wong installed a series of ergonomically correct workstations, along with requisite computers, phone lines, and fax machines. He also had a couch and a television with a videocassette recorder.

"Having the office in my home allowed me to run a business and be an active father," he says. "I could go to my kids' Little League or tennis matches and then come home and check my positions. I was able to work productively at things that were important to me."

Wong believes the convenience allowed him to be not only a better father but a better manager, too. "I can work whenever I want," he said. "I literally can put my kids to bed and be in the office in five minutes looking at reports or scouring the news. I no longer have to carry tons of paper around or spend hours commuting."

Although the community of hedge fund managers and service providers to the industry has been growing quite rapidly in the past few years, it is still relatively small compared to the entire institutional investment community. As such, and as is the case throughout much of Wall Street, many of the industry's players, including the managers, lawyers, and brokers, know each other. Still, as the industry grows many people are not able to keep track of all of the managers and all of the firms doing hedge fund business.

"It used to be that everyone literally knew everyone in this business," says Bill Michaelcheck, chairman of Mariner Invstments, a hedge fund organization profiled in Chapter 3. "Now because everyone and their brother is starting a fund, it is getting harder and harder to know everyone and, more importantly, to know what everyone is doing."

An interesting twist is that many of the marquee names who have been at the forefront of the hedge fund world for decades are slowing down and setting up their children in funds.

Take, for example, Jack Nash, who retired in 1997 from Odyssey Partners and set his son up with a new fund called Ulysses. Michael

Steinhardt, who had been threatening to retire for many years, finally did so in 1995, but he has a son who is running his own fund. In October of 2004, George Soros announced that his two sons, Robert and Jonathon, would become deputy chairmen of Soros Fund Management, which at the time had over $12 billion in assets under management.

According to an article called "The Other Soros" in *Institutional Investor* in March 1998, Robert Soros said he had no pressure or encouragement from his father to enter the business. Rather, George Soros felt it would be hard for Robert to work in a place where his father cast such a big shadow. It would seem that the shadow is fading.

Slowly, the patriarchs of the hedge fund world have passed the torch to the next generation, who no doubt will work very hard to continue the legacy created by their parents.

It was not always as easy to start a hedge fund as it is today. Fifteen years ago, it would have been hard to find a lawyer or accountant who could help. Of course, many knew of the investment vehicles and understood the structure but very few specialized in the industry. That picture changed with the success of the business and many flocked to it, not only as potential fund managers but as supporting players.

Today, many of the main figures in the hedge fund industry work together, and through a network of referrals you can find some of the best legal and financial talent available. It takes just one phone call to schedule an appointment with an accountant, a lawyer, and a prime broker.

"The idea is to provide as much service as we can to the manager in order to make sure we are able to get and hold on to the business," explains an employee at one of the leading prime brokerage firms. "Although hedge funds are a dime a dozen, the key is to work with funds that are going to grow and be successful so that over time the business grows from within instead of relying constantly on new clients."

Many of the service providers, attracted by the industry's expo-
nential growth, market their organizations as one-stop shopping
sources for all the fund managers' needs. At conferences and seminars,
prime brokers team up with lawyers who are connected to accountants who work with third-party marketing agents, all in the name of
service and, of course, the generation of fees.

Experts ascribe the growth of hedge funds to the acceptance by
the investing public of alternative investments and to the fact that
people in general have more dollars to invest.

"There are many people who have a lot more money today than a
few years ago, and they are looking for better returns than they can get in
mutual funds or individual stocks," says a fund manager who recently retired and requested anonymity. "The strength of the economy has not
hurt the industry. When people make millions of dollars through stock
options and initial public offerings, eventually they realize they have to
do something with the money if they want to hold on to it.

"Sure, they can put it in mutual funds or individual stocks, but
they would rather put it into something exotic that may pay better returns and give them something to talk about at cocktail parties," he
continues.

As the market grows, people are looking for investment opportunities that are unique and that will provide them with greater returns.
The ability of a hedge fund to use any means necessary to post increased returns makes it very attractive both to investors and to potential managers.

Over the past few years, a number of independent studies have
shown that, on average, hedge funds post higher rates of return than
those of the S&P 500 and other benchmarks. This ability continually
to outperform the market appeals to potential individual investors
who are looking for higher returns and are not concerned necessarily
with the accompanying higher risk.

Still, there are naysayers who believe hedge funds' ability to outperform the market is overstated.

One of them is George Van, chairman of Van Hedge Fund Advisors, a consultant to potential hedge fund investors, who believes that in some cases the return isn't worth the risk, that many funds barely beat the S&P year after year while taking substantial chances with investors' money. Van believes the key to investing in hedge funds is to find the right fund and, more importantly, the right manager.

Figure 2.1 through 2.3 illustrate hedge fund performance versus both equity and fixed income indexes. The charts show performance numbers for funds with various trading styles and strategies for the period 1999–2004. The data was compiled and supplied by Van Hedge Fund Advisors International LLC.

Veterans of the industry often question the excitement surrounding hedge funds and point to the fact that many of today's managers have never seen a down market. These old-timers question the newcomers' ability to handle the market when it corrects itself.

"It is too easy for people to get into the industry," says Jim Rogers, president of Rogers Holdings and a former partner of George Soros. "When we started out, it was a lot harder and there was nobody around to help us. Now there are brokerage firms, law firms, and

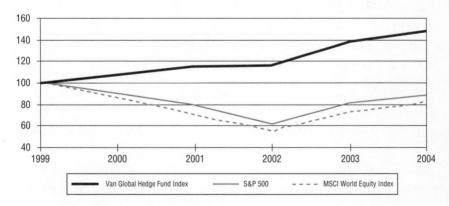

FIGURE 2.1 Van Global Hedge Fund Index vs. S&P 500 and MSCI World Equity Index 100 as of the end of 1999.

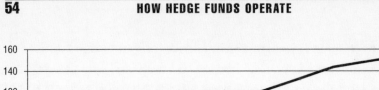

FIGURE 2.2   Van U.S. Hedge Fund Index vs. S&P 500 and MSCI World Equity Index 100 as of the end of 1999.

Copyright 2005 Van Hedge Fund Advisors International, LLC.

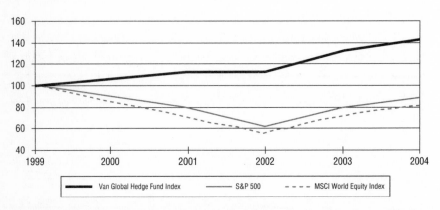

FIGURE 2.3   Van International Hedge Fund Index vs. S&P 500 and MSCI World Equity Index 100 as of the end of 1999.

Copyright 2005 Van Hedge Fund Advisors International, LLC.

accounting firms all specializing in hedge funds, which makes getting into the business easy."

Michael Steinhardt, who had more than 30 years of stellar performance, disagrees with Rogers in that he believes hedge funds *always* have been an easy business to get into. "How many other businesses are there where with just a few years of experience you can hang out your shingle in a relatively unregulated industry and get 20 percent of the upside on other people's money?" he asks. "Ease of entry into the business is extraordinary. It always was but it was a psychic leap for people in the sixties and seventies to invest in hedge funds. Today, everybody wants to run a hedge fund and everybody else thinks they should be investing in one."

What has lowered the barrier in the past 10 years is Wall Street's understanding of how profitable providing services to the hedge fund community can be. The issue now is what happens to the industry when the market cracks.

"Starting a hedge fund is probably the most efficient way to make money in the financial world today," Rogers says. "The problem is once things start to turn, people will lose money and things will get ugly, and when they get ugly, everyone loses."

Today, more than a dozen organizations will assist potential fund managers in drafting legal documents, provide brokerage services, and also help with marketing and money raising.

What makes the whole industry so incestuous is that even when people blow up or self-destruct, they can still find work in it and often are able to profit handsomely from their mistakes. More likely than not they will come back either as money managers or in the form of other cogs on the gears that make the industry spin.

When Victor Niederhoffer's operation blew up in October 1997, people said he would never manage money again. The evening after the morning he was shut down, I was at an industry function talking to one of his investors who, prior to the collapse, had been one of his staunchest supporters. The investor told me that he had never seen anything so ugly, and not everything had been fully disclosed.

"This mess is so big, I don't think he will ever be able to work in this industry again," the investor said. "Nothing can save him."

However, saved he was. Four months later the following ad ran in the *Wall Street Journal*'s help wanted section:

FINANCIAL MARKETS

Wanted: Individual with good quantitative mind, creativity, programming skills and interested in aspects of financial markets to work in a small, innovative, formerly successful trading firm in CT. Must be flexible and willing to learn. Low starting salary, excellent potential. Fax resume to Victor Niederhoffer . . . .[2]

The man who prides himself on reading no newspaper other than the *National Enquirer* was back. But, how? How was it possible to have lost so much and yet come back so quickly? The answer is one part ego, one part stamina, and one part rich friends.

Niederhoffer had proved himself a solid money manager. Like a number of people in the industry today, he insisted on making his story known; he wrote a book, gave many interviews, and was available to anyone who would listen to his story. He was known as someone who could bet heavily on one side of the market only to be wrong and then miraculously recover—a wild trader who performed well in any market condition. He also had some very wealthy friends, or, more accurately, one very wealthy friend: George Soros. It seems that unlike most other areas of Wall Street where you are only as good as your last trade, with Niederhoffer it did not matter. Through his connections he was able to reestablish himself and begin trading again. Niederhoffer would not comment on where the money for his current fund came from, but many in the hedge fund world believe a good portion of it came from Soros.[3]

Another money manager who blew up after losing almost all of her partners' capital by betting on micro-cap stocks has found a niche for herself on the marketing side of the business. After a bit of time spent soul-searching, she set up a firm in midtown Manhattan that specializes in third-party marketing of hedge funds, which means she is helping them to attract investment capital. She works within a network of wealthy individuals, family offices (limited partnerships or limited liability companies), and institutions, helping them decide where to put their money.

"Most hedge fund managers I have met and worked with have two problems when it comes to raising money: Number one, they have no interest in marketing, and two, they don't know how to do it," she says. "My experience in both raising money for my own fund as well as having worked in institutional sales has allowed me to build a network of potential investors that are interested in finding a good manager who has a good strategy and who will provide them with solid returns. I believe that I bring strength to both sides of the equation—I know how to pick good managers and I know how to find money."

Both of these cases illustrate that there is life after death in the hedge fund industry. The Long-Term Capital case presented earlier proves that if you know the right people, you may not have to find work after you blow up.

Before you can blow up, however, you need to create an organization. There are four essential puzzle pieces: money, a lawyer, an accountant, and a prime broker.

Once you find a lawyer, the next item on the list is usually a prime broker, who serves as office manager, back-office support person, and something like an execution clerk. Prime brokers provide almost everything a fund manager needs to get started. Accountants are least important at start-up but most important after the first year, when the accountant brings validity to the track record, one of the most important tools in helping to raise money. And an accountant makes it all official.

As for money, it takes surprisingly little. Most fund managers start out with having enough money in the bank to cover living expenses for a year or two, plus what they have invested in the fund and some for administrative expenses, so that they do not have to worry about where money is coming from to pay bills and live while they are building their business.

One fund manager told me that she waited for almost two years before she launched her fund to make sure she had enough to cover living expenses for at least two years. "I knew it would be a very long time before I would be able to take out any of the money I earned in the fund and live on it, so I knew I had to have a lot of money in the bank to ensure it was not a problem."

She also wanted to make sure that she didn't need any money she did earn from the fund, so that she could invest it right back into the fund and continue to increase her stake.

Some of the most significant costs of doing business are those associated with administering the fund. Administration costs range from data feeds and execution costs to rent and telephone bills. Many new fund managers try to keep these expenses down by working with a prime broker that will provide all the services as part of a package. Once the fund is up and running, though, many managers build elaborate office complexes and install large organizations to run and administer the operation. This is in direct contrast to A. W. Jones, who was often ridiculed by his partners and employees for not wanting to spend money on a large office filled with modern accoutrements.

Prime brokers provide the up-and-coming as well as the established hedge fund manager with everything from execution services and daily profit-and-loss statements to Bloomberg terminals and office space.

Some of today's leading prime brokers are Banc of America Securities, Bear Stearns, Credit Suisse First Boston, UBS Hedge Fund Services, Goldman Sachs and Morgan Stanley. Since operating a hedge fund is very lucrative to the fund's manager, being the prime broker to a successful fund can be very lucrative to the Wall Street firm providing the services.

Since the early 1990s, providing prime brokerage services has been known as Wall Street's "diamond in the rough." The idea is very simple. The brokerage firm provides the hedge fund manager with custody and clearing. As perks, if you will, firms also provide managers with office space, data feeds, phone lines, and everything else they need to run their business. Besides paying a fee for the services, the fund manager and the prime broker have an understanding: The manager will route some of his or her trades through the prime broker's trading desks—which in turn will generate commissions. There is no written agreement that says this nor is there a requirement as to how many trades must be sent to the brokerage firm. That would be illegal. There is, however, an unwritten rule and managers know that if the prime broker does not see some commission dollars, they will be asked to take their business elsewhere.

"For the most part, we get a good share of our customers' business," says Stephan Vermut, the former president and chief executive of Bank of America's prime brokerage unit and now operates Merlin Securities. "We do not force people to trade with us, nor do we expect to see them send every trade through to our desks. We do however expect some orders from the managers."

Vermut said his company usually received 20 to 30 percent of its clients' commission dollars, which he says is the industry norm. Other prime brokers agreed, saying that if a customer does not send at least 20 percent of its trades to the prime broker's order desks, the manager will be asked to look elsewhere for a prime broker.

"Some people do all of their business through us while others do just a fraction," Vermut says. "In the end, the numbers make sense and the business model has worked very well for us."

Remember, it is very easy for the prime broker to keep track of the fund's trades and where it executes the orders because the firm keeps its books and records. On any given day at any given hour the firm acting as a prime broker can look at screens and see which funds are trading with it and which are trading away and immediately determine which relationships make sense.

Although the field of firms providing prime brokerage services is quite crowded, there are a few that stand out. Morgan Stanley Dean Witter is by far the biggest provider in terms of assets under management of prime brokerage services. Bank of America seems to be the fastest growing firm that provides prime brokerage services and through its use of technology—in particular its World Wide Web trade reporting product—many fund managers believe it is the most sophisticated service provider.

In its annual survey of the industry, *Global Custodian* found that some other companies have started to capture market share, including Merrill Lynch & Co. Inc., UBS, Lehman Brothers Holdings Inc., and Daiwa Securities. The survey observed that "prime brokerage is one of the few operationally intensive businesses where brokerage houses are better positioned than banks however that is not stopping banks from stepping up their efforts to service hedge funds."[4]

"It used to be that when you signed on a new client, you broke open a bottle of champagne," says one person who has been in the prime brokerage business since the mid-1980s. "After the crash, the business took off and has never been the same since. Now we can add one or two new clients a month." Instead of bubbles flowing at prime brokers, the money is.

The reason the hedge fund business exploded in the early part of the new millennium was that many on Wall Street realized that their careers and, more important, their bonuses were tied to others. They came to believe it was not worth the risk of losing their jobs because someone else made a mistake.

"By opening up hedge funds they could be their own boss and

know that they did not have to worry about how others performed," says one observer. "They just had to rely on themselves."

Today the prime brokerage business represents a significant piece of revenue for many firms. Goldman Sachs, for instance, which for years said it would not work with managers who were just starting or who managed only a small amount of assets, has changed that policy and will now work with almost anyone. The reason? Nobody knows where the next Soros, Robertson, or Steinhardt will come from. And the firm does not want to miss out on potentially huge sources of revenue that may come down the road.

In the past few years, many of Wall Street's biggest and smallest brokerage firms built their prime brokerage business to the point that it is hard to tell one from the other. The entire franchises are based on technology, especially the order execution systems. All reporting and analytical functions are at a manager's fingertips via the Internet. Not only do the prime brokerage systems store current data, but they also provide historical information. The systems are designed so that a manager does not have to wait for reports to be delivered or to have documents retrieved to get a picture of the fund's situation.

Prime brokerage is such a profitable business that pretty much all of the large, medium, and small firms offer services to budding and existing hedge fund managers. Over the past few years, many firms have been launched to simply provide hedge fund managers with just execution services. One- and two-man trading companies who use third-party software and clear their trades through the large clearing houses are now offering services to budding and existing managers. These shops specialize in order execution at very cheap prices, which means that fund managers can save money on commissions.

And while smaller shops have opened and gotten into the game, larger firms are continuing to expand the products and services that they are offering to hedge fund managers. It used to be that you needed to have significant assets to get into some of the "name" brand prime brokers, now, however, as long as you have some money under management pretty much any of the firms will open an account for you. The business is so lucrative that firms including Fidelity Investments, the large mutual fund company, have in the last few years started offering prime brokerage services to the hedge fund community. Today because the hedge fund industry is growing at such a fast pace and there is plenty of business to go around, most firms operate under the unwritten rule not to poach clients. However, once the market turns and not as many funds are being created, it will be open season and no one's clients will be safe.

"Our business is a safe bread-and-butter business that allows the firm to profit handsomely for providing services while taking very little risk," asserts a person in the prime brokerage industry. "We have never had a situation evolve where we lost money or took a capital hit when a fund blew up. The most we can ever lose is commission dollars. If a fund blows up, we will replace it with another."

Just to be on the safe side, in light of the blow-up of Long-Term Capital and other recent blow-ups and scandals, many firms have begun to aggressively reevaluate their risk exposure to make sure that they do not have too many funds with concentrated portfolios that could pose a risk to the firm's business. According to one prime brokerage executive, the firm's management committee did not understand the services and function that its prime brokerage unit provided to its hedge fund clients and was nervous about the "risks" it was taking in this line of business.

"I have been called a number of times by senior management requesting information about what sort of risks we were taking and losses we should expect when the market turns or a hedge fund blows up," said a risk manager at a large prime broker in New York City, who requested anonymity. "When I told them none, they first questioned if I knew what I was talking about and then thanked me for doing my job so well."

In one room you may have a fund that specializes in special situation equity plays, in another you may find a manager who trades foreign currency options, while a third may simply trade small-cap equities that are linked to the financial services industry. Each has a different strategy and management style, yet some may have the same investors.

Prime brokerage services are just a small part of what is often thought of as a sophisticated world of hedge fund operations. In reality, like most businesses, the fundamentals of operating a hedge fund are quite simple.

In most cases there are just three aspects to the business: marketing and raising capital, legal and accounting work, and investing and trading. Most managers do not want to have anything to do with the first two and therefore farm them out to third parties. In the past few years, managers have found they can pretty much get all of their trades executed and their legal work and accounting functions handled by outsourcing at a fraction of what it would cost to do them in-house.

"Most hedge fund managers have no interest in marketing and, more important, don't have any idea as to how to do it," says Barbara Doran, former managing director of Global Capital Strategies LLC in New York, a third-party marketing firm.

When Doran worked with a fund, her job was to find investors. She promoted the fund and its manager to everyone from wealthy individuals and family offices to corporations and endowments. Doran, like other third-party marketers, was paid a fee for bringing in capital. In most cases the marketing firm works on an exclusive basis just as a real estate broker would if you were trying to sell your home.

In today's competitive marketplace the key to survival is the ability to attract and keep investors. To do so, a manager must put up solid returns quarter after quarter and the marketer must be able to tell likely investors a compelling story.

Many managers run into a catch-22 when it comes to attracting new investors. In most cases, new managers have very little track record of their own and therefore they do not have much muscle behind their story. While traders may have been successful at Goldman or Salomon and received huge bonuses, who is to say what they will do on their own or how much of their success was based on their own effort? Therefore, managers who strike out on their own need to have a large group of contacts and character witnesses who can bring potential investors to the table.

A recent trend in the industry is that of large, established hedge funds and money management firms placing investment dollars with start-ups.

One fund manager that I spoke with had been approached by a number of the hedge fund world's marquee names offering to invest in the new fund. At first the manager could not believe the good fortune. But this situation had a number of strings attached. When the manager sat down with the potential investors' representatives, it turned out the hedge funds wanted to wield a lot of control over investment decisions and wanted to split all of the new fund's fees.[5] The manager decided that although it would be great to have their money in the fund, it would be better in the long run to do without it.

"They wanted too much control and I did not think it would be worth it," the manager explains. "In the short run it would have been nice to have their money, but over time it would have been a problem. It was very difficult to walk away from their money, but looking back I am glad I did."

Many large hedge fund organizations like to give money out to new and smaller managers because they believe it will help them significantly with their performance and, more importantly, help them with idea generation. The idea is simple; there are just so many hours in a day and only so many good ideas that one organization can find but, by farming out some of their money, the large manager is able to expand his or her reach in the marketplace and cast a wider net in search of investment ideas and, more importantly, avoid slippage.

"The new fund managers get a good chunk of money which allows them to get established while we usually get the best years of their performance," he says. "And it helps us avoid slippage." Slippage is the losses that a fund manager creates when he or she tries to move large sums of money in and out of a small position and the market moves before the order is completely executed.

It is very hard to move large sums of money in and out of good investments. A manager who likes a stock that is thinly traded needs to be careful that going in or out does not cause the market for the stock to move significantly. Often even the rumor of a hedge fund's going into a stock can cause market turmoil. Therefore a big fund becomes limited as to what it can and cannot buy. It is a lot easier to find places to invest smaller amounts of money, so by putting money with a new fund, a large fund is able to capitalize on situations that otherwise would not be available.

For the most part, once a manager takes money from another manager, there is a confidentiality agreement that does not let the manager who is receiving the money speak about the fund that is providing it. Of course, as long as it does not appear in print, most managers are willing to give up the name to potential investors because it is a pat on the back. If George Soros or Julian Robertson likes this guy and has given him money, why shouldn't you?[6]

"Many large hedge funds spread the dollars around in order to continually put up strong numbers, and in most cases it is good for young managers who can get these investments. The problem is they can't tell anyone about it," says an industry observer who requested anonymity. "If the world knew that some of the largest funds were doling out money to people who were still wet behind the ears, how do you think that they would react when the performance comes in and they have to pay such a large percent of the profits to people who did not even do any work?"

Regardless of the outside investors, the most important aspect of a start-up fund is the manager's own stake. Even established funds would have a hard time raising money if the manager did not have a significant stake in the fund. Investors are saying to the managers: "Put your money where your mouth is."

A hedge fund is doomed if managers do not have their own money in it. It really does not matter how much, but some managers put every penny they have in their fund.

One manager told me that at one point he was putting so much into his fund that the gas and electric company were threatening to cut off service to his home. His office assistant finally persuaded him to take some money out of the fund to live on, but he says it was difficult because he believed so strongly in what he was doing that he wanted to have as much invested as possible.

As hedge funds continue to become more popular, many future Wall Streeters are going right into business for themselves instead of working for a brokerage firm or hedge fund. A number of funds have been started recently by people in their early twenties who have had some luck in the market, using $50,000 to $100,000 of family money.

One fund manager started his fund while in high school and ran it through four years of college. He told his investors that he would be closing the fund and would liquidate all of its positions by year-end. He wrote in his annual letter to investors: "After serious thought, I have reached the inescapable conclusion that I will not be able to work for somebody else and simultaneously manage [the fund]. After graduation I must just join the real world and find gainful employment."

I wonder if the manager's investors knew he was not in "the real world" while he was investing their "real money" in "real securities," and although he had "real gains" he could instead have had "real losses."

Most hedge fund managers understand that they operate in a real world and that their real careers are on the line based on their investment decisions. This is not always the case with those who cover the industry. The popular press is often quick to criticize managers because they are apt to make a deal when it comes to accepting new investors.

Nobody is forced to invest with a manager. An individual or institution does it by choice. In all cases it is up to the investor to perform due diligence and determine if the manager's investment ideas and criteria mesh with his own investment objectives.

An article in *Forbes* in April 1998 questioned one manager in particular because the minimum investment in his fund was "negotiable" and because he ran the fund out of his apartment in Manhattan.[7]

The same article also questioned famed hedge fund operator Julian Robertson for having lowered his minimum investment to $1 million from $10 million and for requiring new investors to sign an agreement not to withdraw their money "for five years, even if Robertson 'goes insane, dies or becomes incapacitated.' " The story did not mention, however, his stellar track record for the previous 20-odd years or his continuing ability to reinvent his investment strategies. That's what allows him to take advantage of the world's ever-changing economic landscape.

Hedge Fund Regulations and Structures

When Loomis wrote her *Fortune* article, she looked at some of the people who were investing in hedge funds. As can be expected, a list of names was very hard to come by, but she found a who's who of the nation's rich and famous. It includes Laurence Tisch, Daniel Searle, Keith Funston, Deborah Kerr, Jimmy Stewart, Jack Palance, and Rod Steiger. Today the lists of investors (which are even harder to come by) also read like a who's who of the nation's rich and famous.

One hedge fund investor who should be noted is Laurence Tisch. A very savvy businessman, he has had not such good luck with picking hedge fund managers. Although he refuses to comment on whether he still invests in hedge funds, it is widely known that he is an investor in John Meriwether's Long-Term Capital through a company he owns. It is believed that when he heard of the firm's losses, he immediately asked for a redemption and wanted to get what little money he had left out.

Neither Meriwether nor Tisch would confirm this story, nor would Tisch comment on his investment practices. An article in *The Wall Street Journal* revealed that Tisch did have some money invested in Long-Term Capital through Loews Corp. The article says that the Tisch exposure to Long-Term Capital was a result of its purchase of Continental Insurance of New York in 1995. The insurance company had invested $10 million in Long-Term Capital in 1994 and it received a payout in December 1997 of approximately $18.25 million. The company kept $10 million in the fund and saw that get marked down to under $1 million when Long-Term Capital collapsed.[8]

It is also widely known that Tisch did have substantial positions in a number of hedge funds in the 1960s and 1970s that went belly-up. At the time, he was quoted as saying he'd had it with the hedge funds.

My own alma mater, Clark University, is an active investor in hedge funds. According to James Collins, the university's executive vice president for administration and finance, Clark has been investing in hedge funds since 1993. "The university's investment committee decided to invest in hedge funds because we wanted to diversify our risk exposure and work with some of the smartest minds on Wall Street."

Clark has approximately 20 percent of its endowment invested in five hedge funds, all of which use different investment strategies. To find the fund managers, the university relied on a number of existing relationships its board of trustees had with Wall Street. Members of the investment committee as well as university officials meet and talk with the fund managers on a regular basis to keep tabs on the investments.

"The program is working as we thought it would, and we expect to continue seeing absolute returns of 10 percent to 11 percent from the investments," Collins says. "Over time we believe it will prove to be the right investment for the university's money."

In the fall of 2004, JP Morgan Securities Ltd. released a study titled "Have hedge funds eroded market opportunities?" The study looked at the significant growth in the hedge fund industry over the past few years and questioned whether the size of the industry eliminated a manager's ability to find opportunities to exploit in the market. The study concluded that in areas such as fixed income arbitrage and long/short equity there has been an erosion of opportunities as hedge fund managers scramble to find places to deploy their capital. It did find that opportunities existed in areas where few hedge funds where willing to roam including the credit and foreign currency markets. Nonetheless, the study found that it was "too early to write off" hedge funds. The industry did not do well in 2004 as most funds put up barely positive returns through the first ten months of the year but did quite well in the last two months—postelection euphoria. And although hedge funds may or may not offer an opportunity to investors, the industry is still growing at a significant clip. JP Morgan found that through the period of 1990 to 2003 the industry increased fourfold from 2,000 to 8,000 funds. The industry's assets during the same period grew 20 times, from $38 billion in 1990 to $817 billion at the end of 2003. It is expected that by the end of 2008 the industry will consist of more than 11,500 funds with more than $1.7 trillion in assets under management, which would represent a growth rate of nearly 16 percent per year.

Although these numbers seem impressive and represent significant growth in comparison to the traditional side of the investment management business, they are not so big. For example, at the end of 2003, the amount of money invested in the world equity and bond markets was close to $74 trillion. On this basis, hedge fund assets represent just two-thirds of 1 percent of the total assets in the market.

Investor money comes from all sorts of sources today: college endowments, state pension funds, municipalities, corporations, family offices, wealthy individuals and now retail investors.

As recently as 1990, many corporations and other institutional investors shied away from hedge funds, but this situation has changed as more and more people learn of the types of returns they can get.

"Hedge fund investors are no longer an elite core of the world's wealthiest investors," says Steinhardt. "Publicity about sustained superior returns attracted hordes of money into funds. But many of the old funds such as mine had high minimums and were closed to new money. That alone created a certain mystique about hedge fund investing."

Now, however, because of the proliferation of information as well as market forces, hedge fund data and resources are readily available through sources ranging from specialized consulting firms to Web sites. If you type the phrase "hedge fund" into a search engine on the Internet, it will come up with hundreds, if not thousands, of sites that offer some sort of information on the subject.

Another factor that is causing hedge fund information to be more readily available is the change in the regulations surrounding the number of investors.

In 1996, the National Securities Markets Improvement Act quintupled the number of investors allowed in hedge funds to 500. Since hedge funds began in the late 1940s, the total number of investors allowed had been 100. Sometimes fund managers and their lawyers interpreted the law so they could have only 99 investors because they also counted the general partner as a limited partner. However, according to Richard Valentine, a former partner at the law firm of Seward & Kissel, the general partner did not need to be counted.

"People thought that they had to count the general partner as an investor and therefore could only have 99 other slots, but in reality, if they wrote the partnership agreements properly, the general partner did not have to count," he says.

Although the law is pretty clear on limits placed on advertising and marketing—they are not allowed—many fund managers realize that to reap the benefits of the new legislation they need to get their message out. Therefore it is not uncommon today to find an article in the major financial press that touches on hedge funds or focuses on various aspects of the industry. Many managers want to distance themselves from the others and are therefore willing to state their case now more than ever.

A lot of fund managers have also started to become more interested about the world's markets and national economic policies. The Securities and Exchange Commission still does not let hedge fund managers use conventional methods of advertising. Some say this has helped create the mystique of the industry and its managers, while others believe it ensures the safety of unsuspecting investors.

"By not letting fund managers advertise or market their businesses, the SEC has created a veil of secrecy over the industry that really helps the managers attract business," says an industry observer. "People in general are more interested in things that they are told they cannot learn about or do not have easy access to, and therefore it has become easier in some cases for managers to attract investors. People want what others cannot have."

Most of the prime brokers work with their fund managers to help them raise capital. But because the funds are not allowed to advertise, this process can be quite difficult. Often a brokerage firm will put together a report on a number of fund managers, detailing their strategies and performances but without actually naming the specifics. Once investors have the opportunity to review the information, they contact the firm and the firm alerts the manager. The manager then contacts the potential investor. Before any meeting, the manager most likely will put the investor through a suitability test to ensure that they are not wasting time by talking to unqualified investors.

The prime brokerage industry calls this Capital Introduction. It is a service that it provides to its managers to help them market their funds to potential investors. Most firms have Cap-Intro meetings that take place either once a month or once a quarter. The event, which is usually an afternoon, consists of presentations by managers about what they do and how they do it. The idea is to get investors interested in the manger to learn more about the strategy. The meetings are good because a potential investor can literally see four or five managers in an afternoon at one location. In early 2005, the number of Cap-Intro meetings was growing at a very fast pace. It seemed like there was a meeting almost every other week in New York and other major cities.

"The process is hard, but it is the only way we have been able to figure out to market the funds without running the risk of running afoul of the law," says a person who markets hedge funds for a prime broker.

The change in the regulations allows funds to expand the number of limited partners they can have and redefines the guidelines under which an investor must qualify to invest.

accredited investor
an investor who meets the Securities and Exchange Commission guidelines required for investing in hedge funds.

Prior to the change, the only requirement was to be an *accredited investor,* which is defined as someone who has $1 million net worth, including a primary residence, or an annual salary for two consecutive years of $200,000 ($300,000 for a couple) that is expected to continue. While there are set rules as to who can invest in a hedge fund, there are no such rules when it comes to minimum investments. Investments can range from as little as $50,000 to as much as $100 million; it all depends on the size of the fund. Now that the regulations have changed to allow for more investors, the minimums have come down.

The current regulation now allows for 500 limited partners as long as the fund or entity has not accepted any investors who do not meet the qualified purchaser requirements after September 1996. The fund manager has to make it clear in the offering documents that future investors will be limited to qualified purchasers and has to make available to all pre-September 1996 investors the ability to withdraw their investments at net asset value without penalty.

According to Jonathan Baum, a lawyer who specializes in securities law, a qualified purchaser is defined as any trust, natural person, or family-controlled company that owns not less than $5 million in investments, and any person, acting for his or her own account or that of other qualified purchasers, who owns and invests on a discretionary basis not less than $25 million.

"The change in the regulation has been a great thing for large funds that can attract the really high-net-worth individuals and institutions, but for the little guys who can't fill their first one hundred slots, there is no need for this yet," says Peter Testaverde, a partner in Goldstein Golub Kessler, an accounting firm in New York that has a significant hedge fund business. "This whole thing is about the [Securities and Exchange] Commission understanding that people with a net worth of a billion dollars do not need the same protection as Joe Retail when it comes to investing."

Hedge funds for the most part operate as limited partnerships and/or limited liability companies. They are registered as either *onshore funds* or *offshore funds,* allowing for different groups of investors. An onshore fund is open to onshore U.S. taxable investors, and an offshore fund is open to U.S. tax-exempt investors and foreigners.

Today lawyers use boilerplate language for hedge funds' investment memorandums, spelling out to potential investors the structure and strategy of the entity and describing its fund

onshore fund
an investment vehicle that is set up in the United States that is available to U.S. citizens.

offshore fund
an investment vehicle set up outside of the United States and is not available to U.S. citizens' taxable assets.

manager. A potential investor needs to realize that the memorandum is designed to protect the fund manager, so it is very important that potential investors perform their own independent due diligence before investing. Reading the investment memorandum is just a beginning.

Still, there are a number of things that are important to look at when reading an investment memo, including lockup provisions, fee structures, and the type of investments the fund manager plans to make. In most cases, the funds lock up money for one to three years and then allow for withdrawals quarterly. When it comes to explaining what the fund plans to buy and sell, the memos are usually very vague. They say things like, "The manager may use his or her discretion to invest in any or all of the following at any given point in time." The memo will most likely list every single type of security, commodity, or futures contract known to the markets in order to provide the manager with latitude. In most cases, though, managers tend to stick to one or two types of securities or commodities, and that information is usually findable in other areas of the investment memo. The reason for the vague language is freedom. Managers need to have flexibility to invest.

Overall, the best advice for a potential investor is to get help when picking a manager the first or second time. Often that advice comes from other investors. One manager told me that he has a husband-and-wife team that comes off as mild and somewhat naive until they start asking questions about the fund and its investment and management style.

"These sweet old nice people become Attila the Hun as soon as we start talking about money and investment strategy," he says. "A lot of managers think investors are not so smart or with-it, and it is a mistake. If they weren't so smart or with-it, they wouldn't be qualified to invest in hedge funds."

There are many more different groups of investors in hedge funds today than when Jones started out. Some call these investors greedy, but most of Wall Street believes its best and brightest minds are working for hedge funds. If you truly want to beat the market as well as take advantage of various investment styles that are not open to the general public, hedge funds are the only place to put your money, assuming you meet the investment qualifications.

In most cases, plenty of information about funds is made available by the fund operators and their marketing agents. In addition, a number of analytical organizations track the industry. Many funds have Web sites, and managers are often quoted in newspaper and magazine stories. The explosion in hedge funds has also been greeted by an explosion in hedge fund consulting firms. These so-called independent agencies offer potential investors insight into various styles and strategies. The services also provide data and other relevant information on thousands of funds.

In recent years, there have been some questions and a few small scandals regarding the independence of a number of funds. Some independent advisers have been accused of not telling potential investors that they have an arrangement with a hedge fund they recommended and that they receive a fee from it for bringing in new investors. It is not the point of this book to say that these advisers are unethical, but the publisher and the author believe it is our duty to warn the reader of unethical practices by some firms.

The best bet in finding a hedge fund is to use someone you know and trust as an adviser. It is up to investors to understand the type of investment they are getting into, and the only way to do that is to get involved personally.

One aspect of hedge funds that is often confusing is the use of offshore and onshore investment vehicles by fund managers. Many managers have both an onshore fund and an offshore fund, which operate with something called a "master feeder" fund. This structure allows the manager to pool all of the funds' assets in one vehicle that splits gains and losses based on the assets of its onshore and offshore partners.

If, for example, the onshore fund has $60 million and the off-shore fund has $40 million, 60 percent of the profits and losses would go to the onshore fund and 40 percent would go to the offshore fund.

"Using this structure allows the fund manager to make sure everybody gets the same rate of return and they don't have to worry about entering an order and allocating the proceeds," says Testaverde. "It is a cleaner way of doing things and gives everybody the same results."

Many fund managers use offshore funds—which are defined as entities that are not registered in the United States because they want to preserve the anonymity of their investors and to avoid a number of tax issues associated with having a fund registered in the United States. "Going offshore ensures complete investor confidentiality but it also means that the fund cannot accept American taxable investors," says securities law expert Jonathan Baum.

The regulations surrounding hedge funds for the most part end with the number of investors and with the definition of who can invest in the funds. However, in the light of the impending regulation requiring registration, hedge funds will most likely come under much more scrutiny by the SEC and the powers that be in the months and years to come. Now hedge fund managers will be audited by the SEC on a regular basis and will be expected to operate within the strict guidelines of being a registered investment advisor.

It is hard to define exactly what a hedge fund is because the various structures used around the globe by managers are so diverse. The clearest definition comes from *Merriam Webster's Collegiate Dictionary*, which defines the investment vehicle as "an investing group usually in the form of a limited partnership that employs speculative techniques in the hope of obtaining large capital gains."

One very famous fund manager told me that the only definition of a hedge fund that he had ever read that made sense to him was the one by Carol Loomis published in *Fortune* magazine 30 years ago: "A hedge fund is a limited partnership organized to invest in securities, with a partnership structured in such a way as to give the general partners—the managers of the fund—a share of the profits earned on the money."[9]

Loomis went to great lengths to ensure that the reader could differentiate between a hedge fund and a simple limited partnership that makes investments:

> The structure has three main features: first, the partnership arrangement, through which managers of a fund can be compensated in such a way as to leave them highly motivated to do well; second, the use of borrowed money to obtain leverage, [a] technique permitting the fund to take maximum advantage of a bull market; and third, the use of short selling as a hedge, or protection against the bear market.[10]

What is interesting is that many within the industry as well as those covering it define the hedge fund by its investment guidelines as set forth by the SEC. Rather than understanding how the vehicle operates, many reporters and industry observers choose to define the vehicles by who can invest, not by what they do.

When I met with Loomis in the spring of 1998, we discussed her articles and the lasting effects they seem to have on the industry. She says she finds it surprising that in all this time, people still turned to these pieces for information and ideas on how the industry operates and how to get started in it.

According to one industry observer, everybody in New York except the cabdrivers is starting a hedge fund for one simple reason: *money.*

"You are seeing a lot of investment professionals leaving their firms and starting funds because they think that they can make more money by not having to share the P&L [profit and loss] with upper management," he points out. "A lot of research guys and traders are also jumping in because it is a phenomenon that is going to work in good times and bad.

"Many people are looking to invest in hedge funds because they are greedy and want to outperform the market," he continues. "If people were satisfied with the returns of the S&P or the Dow, not only would there not be so many hedge funds but there would be a lot less business on Wall Street."

He believes that the reason hedge funds will grow in bad times as well as good is the egos that put people on Wall Street to begin with: "In good times, people don't want to share profits with the house and they believe they can do it on their own; in bad times a lot of talented people lose their jobs and they have egos large enough to let them go out on their own."

One of the greatest advantages to hedge funds had been the manager's ability to use any means necessary to find profitable places to put money. Now that a number of the most exciting places have once again fallen on hard times and many hedge funds have lost large amounts of money, the number of people who want to exploit these exotic opportunities may be getting smaller.

When a fund goes from having $300 million under management on Friday to having just under $200 million in assets on Tuesday, it's hard to attract new money.

How Hedge Funds Use Leverage

One of the industry's problems is that a lot of managers who find themselves in trouble are not using the Jones model and thus are not running true hedge funds. Most funds today do not hedge as Jones did throughout his career but rather use large amounts of leverage, which allows them to capture enormous gains on even the smallest price movements. Although Jones was a great believer in leverage, he also believed in executing short positions in order to have a cushion in case the market fell out from under him. Many managers only use short positions sporadically and therefore are not protected when things do not go their way. To be protected, a hedge fund needs to have a significant amount of short positions.

Leverage, despite what much of the press thinks, is not a dirty word. Often those who employ a Jones model will use a 70 percent to 40 percent split of long to short positions. Leverage is an important tool that when used properly can boost returns while limiting risk.

A very simple example is the following situation: If a fund is 75 percent long and 25 percent short, the fund is net long 50 percent—a bullish posture in which the shorts have to work three times as hard as the longs. However, through the use of leverage, the same fund could be 125 percent long and 75 percent short, giving the fund, while it is still net long 50 percent, greater protection on the downside. In this example, the shorts only have to work 1.7 times as hard as the longs. This is business school Leverage 101, and it is something not to be feared but to be embraced by both fund managers and investors.

Prior to the blow-up of LTCM, the hedge fund world had been for the most part flying below the radar screens of the world beyond Wall Street. The one aspect that did become quite newsworthy was that a number of the industry's most famous managers had decided to return capital to investors.

These so-called Midas traders have amassed a fortune for both themselves and their partners by doing what they do best: investing money and picking winners. They have also become more realistic in the past few years. There have been many instances where these Midas traders have had to return capital to investors because it was time for them to retire.

"Prior to the market adjustments of summer 1998, the trend for a number of years had been to return capital," says an industry observer. "But, once the hedge fund world digested the losses associated with the market turmoil, people went on a binge to raise capital.

Many managers thought that if they did not raise capital, they would run the risk of losing investors."

Patriarchs of the Hedge Fund World

Over the years, many of the most respected and sought-after hedge fund managers returned capital to investors, stopped accepting new investors, or simply shut down their operations. These managers all came to a point where they believed that either they could not continue to provide the performance numbers that their investors had come to expect or simply believed that they had gotten too big. The situation always seems to be the same: The managers have decided that they will be unable to continue to post as superior returns with the sums of money they have and therefore do not want to risk their performance record with too much money to manage.

In some cases, like Michael Steinhardt as well as Jack Nash and the late Leon Levy of Odyssey Partners, the managers decided that there was more to managing money than they were willing to do at that time and that the best thing to do was to close up shop. While others have decided to give back portions of their assets and continue investing as they have for many years to come, these people decided to get out of the business and pass the torch to relatives or friends.

There have also been a number of instances when fund managers have decided that there's so much opportunity out there that they need to get back some of the money they returned and so reversed course.

One of the most interesting people to have the left the hedge fund community in the past few years is Michael Steinhardt. He got started in the late 1960s with two partners, Howard Berkowitz and Jerold Fine. In the fund's first 14 months of operation it grew 139 percent. By 1970, it had become the nation's largest hedge fund, with over $150 million under management, according to an SEC report on the industry. The report was detailed in May 1971 in a story in *Fortune* magazine written by Wyndham Robertson, the sister of Julian Robertson. Titled "Hedge Fund Miseries," the article says "the fund was the only large fund whose assets rose in the period surveyed by the SEC."

At the time, Steinhardt, Fine, and Berkowitz attributed the rise entirely to performance and not to capital infusion. Other funds, according to Wyndham Robertson, saw a decline in assets under management. Some funds lost as much as 95.4 percent of their assets while others lost as little as 1.2 percent.

In 1995, after more than a decade of threatening, Steinhardt finally called it quits. He says that he did not want to be "an armchair philanthropist" and that he wanted to be active in his pursuits apart from money management. Those pursuits range from horticulture and exotic animals to collecting art and providing ways to pass on secular Jewish values to others through organizations.

Until 1994, his fund had never had a down year. Then his wrong bet on European bonds caused his funds to lose close to a billion dollars in assets under management.[11] At the time he announced that he was closing up shop, one industry observer told *The New York Times,* "He recovered beautifully from 1994, so no one can say Michael Steinhardt quit because he could not cut it."[12] A $1,000 investment with Steinhardt from inception to the date it closed its doors in 1995 would have been worth $462,224.

Steinhardt, Soros, Robertson, Tudor Jones, Bacon, and a number of others have built their businesses into so-called super hedge funds. They have proved that no matter how large they get or what type of turmoil rocks the markets, they have the ability to make money.

Still, there has been some question in the past few years whether some of these super hedge funds have become more asset gatherers than traders, simply because the management fees (about 1 or 2 percent) they earn for dollars under management are so huge.

At its height, it is estimated that the Soros organization managed nearly $28 billion in assets under management. It earned approximately $280 million in management fees alone, before it was paid its 20 percent of the profits it earned on its investments.

In 1998, before the Asian flu, Druckenmiller said that Soros's flagship fund Quantum was up approximately 19 percent. This being the case, the Soros organization's slice of the pie would have been around a billion dollars.[13]

Obviously, the majority of fund managers earn nowhere near that kind of money. But think of it this way: If a fund has between $50 million and $100 million under management and it charges 1 percent plus 20, the manager stands to gross between $500,000 and $1 million just by showing up for work. If managers show up to work and perform, the revenue they can earn from their funds is nearly endless. It is no wonder Wall Streeters are flocking to the hedge fund world.

When the press and others start to question the fees that funds collect instead of explaining why they should be so high, the fund managers start to perform. As fast as the managers report their numbers to anyone who will take them, the stories switch from complaints about fees to questions about how the managers are able to do so well and regularly beat the market.

Before all the negative stories about Long-Term Capital, one of the most awful pieces of journalism about hedge funds ran in the April 1, 1996, issue of *Business Week*. The article, titled "The Fall of the Wizard of Wall Street—Tiger: The Glory Days Are Over," was about Julian Robertson. In the piece, *Business Week* accused Robertson of not being able to put up good numbers and of viciously attacking his underlings with his hot temper and erratic management style. The article also accused Robertson of not making company visits and not having an active role in the day-to-day management of his funds.[14]

An outraged Robertson responded in two ways. First, he posted solid numbers for the year, beating the benchmark S&P substantially; and second he filed a $1 billion libel lawsuit against the magazine and its editors. In a settlement, which was reached in December 1997, *Business Week* was forced to say that its predictions regarding Tiger's investment performance had not been borne out and that it had made a mistake in reporting that Robertson no longer made company visits.[15]

Business Week did not retract its comments about his erratic behavior. Although the altercation proved embarrassing for the magazine in light of the media debacles of 1998, the incident proved to have a relatively minor effect on Robertson's organization.

Most people believe Robertson's vindication came not through the settlement but rather by the performance his funds achieved. His trouncing of the market's benchmarks seemed to prove that the entire thesis of the article was wrong. His returns of over 56 percent for the year showed the world that not only was he still in the game but he was better than ever.

Other managers have acted similarly when faced with questions about their ability to manage money and the fees they get for doing it.

Michael Steinhardt told me that one of the things that bothered him the most when he retired was the press's reporting that he did not have a "high-water mark," or a clause in the partnership agreement that says if the fund loses money, the manager will not be paid the incentive fee until it recoups the partners' losses. Steinhardt's fund did not have this clause in the agreement, and the press spent a lot of time writing about that fact when he reported that the fund had lost money for the first time and then announced its subsequent closure.

"While it may now be common industry practice to have a high-water mark, frankly there was no such thing as common industry practices back in 1962," he says. "Hedge funds were not an industry like people talk about them today. It struck me as a bit unfair that the only time the high-water mark issue came up was in 1994, the one year I lost money, 27 years after I started my fund."

Steinhardt says, "There are two sides of a coin. Anybody after a year can leave, and if you stay in when someone is down, you are in essence saying that you believe in the manager. You do not make the judgment based on if the fund manager has a high-water mark or not; you make it based on if you believe in the manager and his investment abilities. My performance record after 27 years in the business stands up as a testament to what I achieved; my business should not have been blackened by some nuance of the partnership agreement."

As many famous hedge fund managers retire and move into more active private lives, a new group of Midas traders is emerging. These men and women are beginning to stake their claim and make their fortune in the industry.

People like Jeffrey Vinik, the dethroned king of the Fidelity Magellan mutual fund, started a hedge fund in 1996 and in his first year made an astounding 100 percent. His fund went from $800 million under management to $1.6 billion. In late 1998, the fund had over $2 billion under management. Many believe his success was made possible because his hands were not tied by regulations that were placed on him when he managed Magellan.

Imagine what would have happened if Vinik had been able to perform as well as the manager of Magellan as he did with his own fund. Not only would there have been a lot more happy investors but most likely Vinik would not have been able to earn as much money. At Fidelity, he did not earn as lucrative an incentive fee nor did he have such a substantial stake in the fund. While on his own, he has both.

By 2000, Vinik had decided he had enough of managing other people's money and decided to close his fund. At the time he announced the closing in the fall of 2000, the fund had grown to over $4 billion in assets under management. During the four years he ran Vinik Partners, launched in late 1996, he racked up a total return of 646 percent before fees versus 110 percent for the S&P 500. In his twelve-year career running money for Fidelity and on his own, he racked up nearly 32 percent for his investors.

Other hedge fund comers who will no doubt reach great heights

include Andrew Fisher, formerly of Salomon Brothers, and Cliff Asness, formerly of Goldman Sachs. Even a manager of Harvard University's endowment, Jon Jacobson, has gone out and started his own
fund. Unlike some of the younger fund operators, these former "Masters of Their Own Universe" are able to attract large sums of money
from the start—making their new business ventures very lucrative
right from the get-go.

It was reported that when Jacobson left Harvard, he took with
him not only his money but also a check for $500 million of the en-
dowment to manage for the university. Out of the gate he was making $5 million—not including his incentive fee. In Vinik's first year
of operation, his firm's total pay package is estimated at over $168
million. Not bad for an operation that has fewer than 50 people
working for it.

With all this money at stake, it's no wonder that hedge fund
managers catch the blame for the world's financial ills.

Hedge Funds Take All the Heat

Today, both television and print journalists are enamored with hedge
funds and with the people who run them. Every time an indicator, be
it the Dow Jones Industrial Average or the Thai baht, moves in a direction that is unfavorable to the masses, journalists blame it on hedge
funds. In recent years, political leaders have also started to blame
hedge fund managers for their countries' market woes.

In 1997 when the Asian currency crisis hit, the first people to be
blamed were not the central bankers or the corporate leaders, but the
men and women who run private investment partnerships in the
United States and abroad.

This was also the case in 1992 when a crisis occurred with the
exchange rate mechanism of the European monetary system. It also
happened in 1994 when international bond markets went into a

tailspin. With each crisis there is blame, and in each case the blame was placed on hedge fund operators. Journalists and government leaders alike blamed hedge fund managers for wreaking havoc for the simple benefit of posting higher returns.

And while over the last few years the press and powers that be have not blamed hedge fund managers for causing crises in the markets, in 2003, the SEC and the Attorney General of the State of New York completed their investigation of a number of hedge funds, finding that they had worked with mutual fund managers to exploit market efficiencies through a practice called mutual fund timing. Once again, hedge funds had been blamed for the ills that occur in the marketplace. This time, however, they were not blamed for destroying market value or attempting to collapse a regime but rather were accused of taking advantage of arbitrage opportunities that existed only by circumstance. Unlike other scandals that rocked the hedge fund community, this time these managers did not act alone in search of profits but rather were in cahoots with the mutual fund industry, and both hedge fund and mutual fund managers were proved guilty of wrongdoing. Since the mutual fund timing scandal, many mutual fund organizations have been hit with substantial fees and been forced to retire many of their senior executives. In the case of Strong Funds, the firm was forced to sell itself and its founder, Richard Strong, accepted a lifetime ban from the mutual fund industry and agreed to pay $60 million. His 30-year-old firm agreed to a $115 million fine for its wrongdoing.

It is extremely hard to prove that the hedge funds are a cause of these financial disruptions. A number of studies have been published recently that show that, except in one or two cases, when a hedge fund was blamed for a financial crisis it was not at fault. Most of the time the hedge fund gets caught in the middle—although, in light of the Federal Reserve's action regarding Long-Term Capital, many would find this argument hard to believe.

Case in point: In the summer of 1998, the Russian markets nose-dived. Many people believe it was caused by the Asian crisis while others thought the causes were corruption and the inability successfully to move to a capitalist market system. In the early part of the crisis, in the last week of August, the investment manager of the largest hedge fund organization in the world announced that his funds had lost over $2 billion in Russia. Subsequently, many managers came out of the closet and publicly announced that they had lost significant amounts of capital because of the crisis. Although these announcements came as a surprise to many and offered a rare glimpse into the profits and losses of some the world's most successful money managers, for the most part people did not seem to care. Some people were probably happy and believed that these Midas traders got what they deserved.

If these men and women were so powerful that they could control currencies and markets, wouldn't they do so all the time so that they could always make money? No matter how much or how little money one has, no one likes to lose it. If the funds could truly control currencies or manipulate the markets, these massive losses would not have occurred. Instead, these Midas traders were reduced to mere mortal status and joined the ranks of countless other money managers who have made mistakes and proved that they are truly only human.

The *Economist* magazine believes the reason hedge funds catch flak for all of the world's financial crises is ignorance.[16]

The so-called buccaneers, gunslingers, and highwaymen of the global economy have been blamed for everything from the fracturing of Europe's exchange rate mechanism in 1992 and the crash of the Mexican peso in 1994 to the destabilization of East Asia's currencies in 1997 and the collapse of the Russian ruble in 1998.

Although hedge funds as an industry were attacked for these misfortunes, one person in particular was singled out by a number of finance ministers as being the sole reason for the most recent currency crisis: George Soros.

Around this time, headlines around the world cited Soros Fund Management as the reason for the collapse of the Thai baht and other Asian currencies. Malaysian prime minister Mahathir Mohamad blamed Soros and "his Jewish counterparts for getting together and deciding which country's economy to destroy." According to press accounts, the prime minister believed Soros et al. achieved these goals by simply making trades that they know would cause this to happen. The problem with this theory was that hardly anybody besides the prime minister subscribed to it.

Soros and his colleagues were vindicated by a report issued by the International Monetary Fund (IMF) as well as by statements by then U.S. Secretary of the Treasury Robert Rubin. During a four-nation tour of Asia in the summer of 1998, Rubin said that he did not blame speculators for the Asian financial crisis and that he opposed controls that some countries had urged to restrict their activities. "The role of the speculators will be found to have been relatively small and transient," he says. "I don't think [their trading activity] has been principally or centrally involved in what happened to currencies."[17]

Some believe that Rubin's comments were especially helpful in weakening the growing storm against hedge funds because of his previous role as cochairman and manager of the highly profitable currency trading unit at Goldman Sachs Group LP. "People think he knows about trading and markets because of his former life and they respect what he has to say," says one industry observer. "When someone who used to be in the markets speaks about what is going on in the markets, their voices are heard and their statements for one reason or another always seem to make sense."

The hedge fund world's real vindication came, however, in the form of a study by the IMF in the summer of 1998. It made the Malaysian prime minister and those few who subscribed to his beliefs look silly. The report, "Hedge Funds and Financial Market Dynamics," surveyed fund managers over a period of six months, and looked at their trading activities on both a macro and a micro level. Some of its conclusions proved to be the opposite of what was the popular belief regarding the role of hedge funds in currency markets. In most cases, the IMF found that when a hedge fund bet on a currency, it brought stabilization to the situation instead of destabilizing it. The study determined that hedge funds were not the only ones to take large positions that bet on the baht's devaluation in 1997. The herd of traders betting on devaluation was led by other commercial and investment banks as well as Thai companies, the report concluded.[18]

The baht situation is not the only currency crisis the IMF reviewed. The study found that many large hedge funds bought substantial positions in the Indonesian rupiah only to lose significant amounts of money when the currency fell from its previous lows.[19] Therefore, the exact opposite of the Malaysian prime minister's remarks seems to be true regarding hedge fund collusion on devaluation of the world currencies.

The IMF study also looked at a number of issues surrounding the most recent financial crises and found that in each episode, the hedge funds seem to have made the situations more stable, not less so. According to the study, because of the "little concrete information" available about the trading patterns of the various hedge funds that were looked at, there is no way to determine what, if any, role they played in these crises. Still, through their efforts to post strong returns they often sell currencies short when a country's macroeconomics look questionable.[20] Although shorting a currency may seem bearish, in reality it is bullish because eventually the position has to be covered by the short seller. If a hedge fund shorts a currency, it is betting on its getting weaker initially. Yet the manager knows that it will have to be bought back, and most likely plans to ride it to new highs on the upside.

The IMF determined that even if the largest hedge funds did all move together or "herd," the scope of their investments would not be anywhere near that of other institutional investors simply because the others have more money.

"The amount of money these macro hedge funds control is relatively small compared to institutional investors," says Barry Eichengreen, one of the authors of the IMF study. "Hedge funds do not stack up against banks, corporations, and pension funds, which engage in the exact same kind of speculation. The hedge funds are more vocal and in the spotlight more than multinational corporations or money center banks."

Eichengreen's comments were echoed by former Federal Reserve chairman Paul Volcker. "Hedge funds are a convenient symbol. They move money around fast for quick gains and everybody thinks they are important players in the markets, but in reality they are nothing but a minor factor," he says. "The flows of money come from insurance companies, banks, and other institutions that move from one market to another to cover expenses and make profits. When the markets get upset and become filled with turbulence, it is not the hedge funds' fault; it is the fault of poor economic policy."

No matter how many times Volcker or his peers say it, many still do not believe it, and these nonbelievers continue to blame hedge fund managers for their economic woes.

The carnage of 1998 might have made Volcker's comment clear to many more had the Federal Reserve not been involved with the bailout of Long-Term Capital. The losses that many funds sustained in the wake of the currency and equity crises worldwide were staggering.

George Soros— The World's Greatest Investor

To understand how finance ministers around the globe came to the conclusion that hedge funds are to blame, we need to look at where and when the ill will toward hedge funds started. The finger-pointing started in the wake of the devaluation of the British pound in 1992. It was after this incident that George Soros become known as the world's greatest and its most feared investor.

Soros's efforts netted his fund more than $985 million, truly an incredible bet and enough to make him the world's greatest investor. What most people overlook when they discuss this situation, however, is the amount of risk involved in the bet. It is estimated that at the time he put on the trade, he had more than $10 billion at risk. Had he made a mistake, he most likely would have been wiped out. He bet the ranch and he won.

The story begins in 1990 when Great Britain decided to join the new Western European monetary system. At the time, according to Robert Slater's unauthorized biography, *Soros: The Life, Times, and Trading Secrets of the World's Greatest Investor,* Soros did not think it was a good idea for Britain because its economy was not as strong as the new united Germany's and therefore would be at its mercy.

Under the European monetary system agreement, Britain was to maintain its exchange rate of £2.95 to the German mark. As its economy continued to get worse, the pound faced increasing pressure, but because of the agreement, Britain was unable to move. Throughout the summer of 1992, John Major's Tory government assured the world that the pound would recover and that devaluation was not an option.

Soros, according to Slater, thought this to be nonsense and believed that the situation was a lot worse than the Conservatives thought. By mid-September, the Italians, facing mounting economic pressures of their own, devalued the lira, albeit within agreement guidelines. This was the beginning of the end for the system's ability to determine exchange rates. The actions by the Italians set in motion the trade that has made the name George Soros known in all corners of the world.

On September 15, 1992, Major's government announced that Britain was pulling out of the European rate mechanism and in turn devaluing the pound. The news rocked currency markets around the globe. Traders were sent running to cover their positions in a desperate effort to limit losses. One trader, however, was laughing all the way to the bank. Before the announcement, Soros had sold $10 billion in sterling. When the news broke, his hedge fund racked up almost $1 billion in profit. One trade, one man, one hedge fund.

From that point on, the world has never looked at hedge funds or George Soros in the same way again. The world now saw these once-obscure investment vehicles as forces to be reckoned with—traders who had the Midas touch.

Chapter 3

The Managers

I t is now time to meet some hedge fund managers. These are people from all across Wall Street who have decided that they no longer want to work for a brokerage firm or investment bank but would rather pursue an entrepreneurial existence. Seven unique managers are profiled in this chapter—managers who for the most part you will not read about in *The Wall Street Journal* or the popular press. These managers all use a different investment style and I believe are a good representation of the industry. The idea behind choosing these people is to illustrate the depth of talent in the hedge fund world—and to provide examples of how various managers operate their funds and what types of strategies they employ to have solid performance while working to preserve capital.

The following pages tell the stories of these seven fund managers. A few readers may know some of them, because they have been around for a number of years, but the managers all have one thing in common: They fly below the press's radar screen. For the most part, these men and women are not called for comments or interviews when a crisis breaks or a boom hits. In some cases, it is the first time the manager has agreed to be interviewed. Although each focuses on a different field of investment and their assets range from $2 million to well over a few billion dollars, they all have the same goals—to preserve capital and let profits run.

In the first edition of this book, which was published in 2000, I profiled ten managers from across a series of investment strategies and styles. Since then, six of the ten have either gone out of the business of managing money, have merged their funds with other like-minded funds, or have given back all of their client assets and are simply managing their own money in a strategy similar to that used in their hedge fund. In talking to these people it has become increasing clear that although managing a hedge fund is a great opportunity that can provide significant riches, it is also extremely tough.

"I never knew how hard it was going to be when I got started," said one manager who asked not to be identified. "I thought all I had to do was get the documents done, open an account, hang a shingle, and, poof, the money would start rolling in. Boy was I wrong." This particular manager never had much success raising money and that, coupled with mediocre at best performance, caused him to close his fund after eight years and look for a job. "I never thought I would have to work for someone again," he said. "Now I have to put together a resume, go on interviews, and hope somebody hires me." It has been more than six months since he shuttered his fund and he has not found a job. "It is really tough out there," he said. "There are a lot of people who are in the same boat as I am and a lot more who are about to get in with us."

There are no hard-and-fast statistics when it comes to how many funds open and close each year, but it is a lot. Any hedge fund lawyer or accountant will tell you that business is better than ever and that it does not look as though there will be a drought of new business any time soon. A lot of funds are going out of business.

One hedge fund accountant told me that nearly 10 percent of the funds that his firm audited in 2003 will not be coming back for an audit in 2004. He said that this situation is a direct result of them not being able to raise money and support the overhead that it costs to run a hedge fund. "These people without a track record who don't come out of a large well-established firm like Goldman or Morgan get a real swift kick in the gut when it comes to trying to raise money," he said. "They think that the money is coming off trees because they see stories in the paper about this pension fund and that pension fund allocating money to funds. What they don't realize is that 5,000 other people have seen the article, half of them have semidecent track records and that there is no way, shape, or form that they are going to get the money."

The problem is that all the budding hedge fund managers read about in the popular press are the stories about the fund managers who launch their funds with a few hundred million or a few billion. They never read about the guy with $2 or $5 million who is struggling to pay bills, hire staff, and manage money and can't do it, so after a year or two he folds the tent and goes home. I am not crying poverty to you on behalf of any manager previously profiled and/or otherwise who could not make it. Most have had very successful careers on Wall Street and were doing very well for themselves when they decided to open their own shops. However, they did get a dose of reality and have since had to look for careers or opportunities elsewhere. In the end they all learned one important lesson: Managing money is hard, raising money is harder. In Chapter 4 you will read about a third-party marketer who raises money for new and existing funds. If you are planning on starting a fund, it is definitely something you will want to read.

So what are managers to do? The answer is to dig in, develop a plan, be willing to adapt the plan and go with the flow of the market, and, of course, hope for the best.

Judy Finger and Doug Topkis— Haystack Capital LP

Judy Finger and Doug Topkis like to tell investors that the work they do trying to find investment opportunities is like looking for a needle in a haystack and thus the name of their firm is Haystack Capital LP. The fund, which is based in New York and was started in October 2003, specializes in finding the undiscovered "gems" that for some reason or another Wall Street as a whole has either overlooked or simply not found yet. Looking for these needles seems to be paying off. The fund was up 9 percent in 2003 and just under 30 percent in 2004 compared to the S&P 500 which was up over 12 percent in 2003 and just under 11 percent in 2004. Through the first month of 2005 the fund was relatively flat compared to the S&P which was down almost 2.50 percent.

Finger and Topkis sort of met along the way when they were both independently managing money and seemed to be interested in many of the same stocks. "We found that we think alike, and once we began to share ideas about buying stocks, we found that we had the same style," said Finger. "Although we were not working together at the time, we were both on the buy side and found that we had a real passion for buying small undiscovered companies."

What drew the two together to launch Haystack was that they found that they looked at things the same way; they understood the same catalyst that would drive a stock up and what would bring the rest of the world to "the party," which would push the stock higher. When they looked at each other's personal accounts they found that they owned similar stocks and began to realize that it made sense for them to work together. "We started out by doing joint conference calls, meeting the management of companies together and while we did not come together as a team until October of 2003, we always had fun through the investment process working together," she said. "It got to the point when we decided that one and one makes more than two and we should build a team and start something."

Finger and Topkis believe that they are stock analysts first and business analysts second. This means that just because something is good business, it does not necessarily mean that it will be a good stock. They believe that their edge is that they understand what makes a good stock. The research process includes looking at fundamentals and technical indicators along with searching for a catalyst that will propel the stock higher. They have to understand the stock's liquidity, who owns it, who might own it, and if there is any visibility in terms of analyst coverage. Once they have all this information, they put it all together and determine if the stock is worthy of their fund's assets.

"Our job is to buy things that make sense before the rest of the Street realizes that they make sense," Finger said. "Or vice versa, if we think that the stock is a good short because everybody likes it, we will sell it."

The investment process comes from idea generation and, like most managers, they try to look under every nook and cranny to gather as much information as possible about prospective investment ideas. Literally thousands of stocks would fit their initial screen and they believe that they have to be familiar with hundreds of them in order to keep up. The idea is to identify the change that will come to the stock. Change is the catalyst that pushes a stock that they might have liked before but watched to something that they might actually own. They define catalysts as things that cause significant change to the business, for example, selling off a division or creating a distribution channel. In either case, and there are literally dozens, the catalyst is something that will affect the bottom line of the business.

"We are always reading news and looking for nuggets of information that will cause the Street to revalue the stock and in turn present us with an opportunity," Finger said. "We are constantly looking for change for mispriced opportunities."

Once they find an idea that makes sense, they run it down by gathering as much information as possible about the company, its management, its market share, and its competitors in order to decide if it should go into the portfolio. "We try to talk to everybody we can including some of the regional brokerage firms who we think have really good research teams, focused on local companies," she said. "In some cases, the regional firms may only cover five or six companies but they know the companies better than anyone else and are really good in the names and we want to get as much as we can from them in order to make a better decision."

Topkis and Finger also work closely with the independent investor relations firms to get into the flow of information about their clients and their clients' competitors.

The flow of ideas starts by doing technical screens and then moves into a flow of fundamental information gathering. Their fundamental research is similar to that of other funds; they read the filings, follow the news, meet with the managers, and try to really get the information about the firm in order to make a good decision. They also read the message boards on the Internet about existing and future positions.

"It is absolutely important to read the boards and see what people are saying about a company," said Topkis. "Sometimes you get a disgruntled employee who is looking to tell the world what they know while other times you get a satisfied employee who wants to tell you what good things are going on." The key is to know each side of the story to determine what your risk is and to always know what the downside is of every stock you own. And according to Topkis and Finger, the only way to do that is to come up with every different scenario that could possibly affect a stock price and try to understand them all completely.

"There is no set amount of research that goes into a position," he said. "We may have known about a company in the past, understood the story and decided to wait for the catalyst before we moved and then when it hit moved fast, while others are completely new to us and need to be thoroughly researched."

Just because something is an interesting story does not make it worthy of their assets, the pair said. "In some cases a company looks good but there may be something wrong, too much debt or a problem with management," he said. "Then boom, they retire the debt or hire new management and now the stock makes sense to be added to the portfolio."

The previously described situations are easier for the pair to get into because they already know the company and were simply looking for a catalyst to get into the stock. But, a considerable amount of work goes into the investment process and decision before capital is deployed into a totally new company that they had not been following.

"The process is the same regardless of the company—it just depends on how well we know the company and what research we have already completed when we see the catalyst occur," he said. If the company is brand new, the process can take a day, a week, a month, or longer, depending on how critical they think the situation is and how fast they want to move. "We have to come up with what we believe is an appropriate evaluation and a lot of work goes into that," said Finger. "There is a lot of due diligence that goes into names before they get into the portfolio."

While the fundamentals are important, the pair also likes to own stocks that look good technically.

"It is all about the risk–reward and what is our downside and what is our upside," said Finger. "Sometimes it takes time and we have to wait for something to pull back for us to enter into the position. It is all about our decision analysis."

Many of the companies that Haystack owns have little or no research coverage, small institutional ownership, and low liquidity. "We try to figure out what is going to wake the Street up to the company and buy ahead of it," she said. "We want to be positioned and know what is coming in order to turn the excitement on."

They are always trying to find the gem and build a position appropriately before the discovery happens. "Sometimes it is hard to be early, but at the same time, we need to always be able to react and to not look where it is coming from but look to where it is going," she said.

Haystack builds its positions around companies with a market capitalization of between $100 million and below a billion. On the short side, however, they look at everything. They run on average about 25 positions in the portfolio and limit the size to 4 percent of assets under management. In February the firm had over $100 million in assets under management and was running approximately 50 percent net long. "It would be very rare for us to find 25 names that are worthy of 4 percent," said Topkis. "If we did, we would probably go on vacation."

One example of a Haystack name is Parlux Fragrances Inc. which trades under the symbol PARL. The company, based in Fort Lauderdale, Florida, creates, designs, manufactures, distributes, and sells fragrances and beauty-related products marketed primarily through specialty stores, national department stores, and perfumeries around the world. The company produces the products under license agreements with groups like Perry Ellis, Ocean Pacific, Fred Hayman Beverly Hills, 273 Indigo, and Jockey. In 2004, its big coup was getting the fragrance license for Paris Hilton and Guess products.

Topkis found the company in 2003. He really liked its story but felt that some of the catalysts were far off, so they shelved the idea. Three months later, the company was coming back into the city and the pair decided to look at it again. At this meeting they saw an incredible opportunity. The company was generating significant free cash flow and was on the verge of launching the Paris Hilton and Guess products, which represented significant revenue opportunities.

Over the summer of 2004, they started to amass a position in the stock for the fund. "Other people did not see it and they were literally throwing the stock out," said Finger. "The company was trading at nine times earnings and had initiated a stock buyback program and the stock continued to go down. It was stock that we liked that nobody cared about. It made a lot of sense." By the end of the summer, the stock stopped sliding and started to climb. They got in at $9.00 and saw it run to $24.00. It turned out to be a perfect example of a Haystack model.

One stock that started out a perfect example of the Haystack model but turned against the pair is Natural Health Trends Corp., which trades under the symbol BHIP. Natural Health Trends is a Dallas, Texas–based multilevel marketing firm that sells health products. "For years, the Street hated companies like this but slowly they began to clean up their acts. During the recession a few years ago, a lot of unemployed people found these companies and went to work for them. This caused the companies to grow significantly because they had a lot more salespeople in the field," said Finger. "The returns are quite good, there is very little overhead, and this was a good little company that was trading at $5.00 whose business was about to explode."

They bought the stock at $5.00, sold it at $10.00, and instead of taking the money and moving onto the next stock, they decided to get back in at $20.00 per share. "There was a significant increase in order flow and we thought that they were on track to do $2.00 a share in earnings, and then it all fell apart," she said. "We thought it was going to continue to grow but instead it just fell apart and we took a hit."

The problem was that there were some risks that they did not completely understand, specifically in the company's operation in Asia. It turned out the company had a large business in Hong Kong that was illegally selling in China. Its operation there was shut down. "We were blindsided by the news and the position was cut in half," she said. "The only thing to our credit was that we kept the position small and we had sized it for the risk."

In order for the fund to continue to be successful, the pair operates in a constant state of research; they are always meeting with managers, attending conferences and trying to find new opportunities for investment. "On average we are meeting with five to ten companies a week," said Finger. "This is what we need to do in order to feed the fire or add tools to our toolbox."

After every meeting the pair puts the company into the following decision tree:

- Do we like it and need to start the research process?
- Do we put it on the back burner and check on it in a few months?
- Do we hate it and see no opportunity?

In each case from this decision tree, they then either begin the process or move onto the next potential opportunity. It does not seem like they will be going on vacation anytime soon. Instead, they are continuing to do research and meeting with companies in order to truly find that needle in the haystack.

David Taylor and Mike Williams—Cover Asset Management LLC

There are liquid markets and then there are liquid markets. Managers who trade large-cap stocks and U.S. treasuries operate in liquid markets. However, nothing is as liquid as the foreign exchange (forex) market. Trading forex is truly trading the largest most liquid markets on earth. The foreign currency markets are open around the clock every day of the year. There is always someone willing to buy or sell a currency.

David Taylor and Mike Williams, who run Summit, New Jersey–based Cover Asset Management, specialize in foreign exchange. Launched in February of 2004, their fund is a currency-only fund that allows the managers to focus in this specific area of the world's markets to provide value to investors by exploiting opportunities in the major and minor currencies around the globe.

Together the pair has been working in and around foreign exchange markets for more than 30 years. Several years ago, they realized that it would be profitable and fun to run their own fund. In August of 2003, they launched Cover the firm, at first trading their own money, and then the fund trading money for clients. "The opportunity to start our own hedge fund presented itself about a year and a half ago and we both thought it good to go out on our own," said Williams.

Taylor and Williams employ a short- to medium-term discretionary trading strategy that uses a combination of technical and fundamental analysis to exploit opportunities in the market. "We have a technical model that we developed over the years that we use as an overlay to our fundamental research to give us ideas to execute," said Taylor.

The foreign exchange markets, although lucrative, can also be extremely volatile. In addition to putting on dynamic hedges, one way the fund tries to dampen the volatility is to stick to strict drawdown limits. On any given month the fund limits its drawdown to a 4.5 percent stop loss on the total fund and a 1 percent stop loss on any given position. This means that if a trade goes against them, they limit the downside in order to protect capital. "By having these rules in place, we are able to limit our losses," said Taylor.

The technical model uses a series of signals based on a scale of one to ten. Ten is a strong signal while a one is a weak signal. They start looking at a potential opportunity when the signal comes in at a six. The signals are generated by a number of factors or information in the marketplace such as the convergence or divergence of a currency's moving average. "By using technical indicators, we can get a strength signal in a specific market and from there we can run our fundamental process to determine if the trade makes sense or not," said Taylor. "A signal tells us if the currency is overbought or oversold."

On the fundamental side, they look at global macro issues, geopolitical issues, and regional economic issues to determine the strength or weakness of a currency. "Our trading system is a combination of things that we have worked over the years but it is not a pure black box system," said Taylor. "By using the system in conjunction with the fundamental analysis, we think we can find opportunities that others miss."

The strategy is based on exploiting opportunities, which means that they may have a fundamental view and then take a look at the technical or they may get a technical signal and then look at the fundamentals. Because they are always looking to generate alpha, they do not limit or box in how they do their research. They also look for trends that appear during the technical analysis portion of their research. Once the moving averages start to move and they begin to cross over, they try to identify a trend and get into a trade. "If when we do the research we find that both the technical indicators and the fundamental research look good, we will then put a trade on," Taylor said. "Once the research is complete, we then look at the strength or weakness of the signal to determine what size position we should put on."

Their experience tells them that trends come and go and that sometimes a trend is not a trend but rather a small blip. "It is tough to say when we are in a trend and therefore we keep doing the research until we find something that we think will work," Taylor said. "It really depends on the market and our view as to if it is ready to move or not. There is not one thing that we do that tells us how to act; it is really a combination of things."

Taylor and Williams trade currencies in the cash and option markets. On average the fund will hold a cash position for a couple of days to a few weeks while they use options for longer positions that last between a few weeks and a few months. The portfolio usually consists of four to five positions, which represent 10 to 30 percent of the assets under management. The fund is not limited to which currencies it can trade but the majority of its positions are in the G-10 which includes the U.S. dollar, the British pound, the Japanese yen, the Swiss franc, and the euro. They also look at some exotic currencies as well including the Mexican peso, the Thai baht, and the South African rand.

"Whenever you trade a currency, you are going long one currency and short another," said Taylor. "This means that you are always hedged because you are making a decision as to the strength or weakness of a currency in relation to one another."

Taylor believes that although he has expertise in a number of currencies, he knows very well the Swiss franc. "Over the course of my career, I have developed a lot of relationships and have built up a lot of experience in the Swiss franc," he said. "Because the economy is relatively small, you can really get an idea of what is going on in the central bank area of the country, and it has become a nice proxy for me to what is going on in the world. It gives me a good indication of what is going to happen with other currencies as well."

The currency markets are the largest and most efficient markets in the world and are traded by those speculating on currency, those using them for transactional business and central banking functions. Speculators take by far the largest percentage of business that is traded through the markets on any given day. With the dawn of the euro in January 2002 and the loss of twelve currencies, many thought the foreign currency business as a speculation strategy would be gone within a few years. However, just the opposite has occurred. Since its launch, the volume of transactions in euro has become significant and the liquidity in the currency is enormous, which provides fertile ground for opportunity.

"As a hedge fund manager, we need to be able to adapt and find opportunities regardless of markets or market conditions," said Taylor. "With the euro there has been the emergence of currencies that prior to its launch we would not have looked at because we were focused on other currencies that we were familiar with."

Taylor is referring to the Australian dollar, the Canadian dollar, the New Zealand dollar, and the Mexican peso.

"Basically, you have a marketplace where banks, hedge funds, and individuals are betting on the direction of currency movement in time frames dealing from a one-minute period to a ten-year period," said Taylor. "Within that group you also have what we call the real money flows, corporations who are hedging their currency exposures like when BMW sells cars in the U.S. and needs to repatriate that money back to Germany. In all, the markets turn over on average about $3 trillion dollars a day."

Most of the trading that Cover does is spot trading. Spot trading is the purchase or sale of a currency that will settle in two days after the trade date. For example if they want to go short the dollar versus the euro, they will buy euros with dollars. It is very rare that they actually deliver in the currency or cash because for the most part, hedge funds like Cover trade on margin. This means that they keep balances at the prime broker or custodian bank to cover the trade but that they can freely operate in and out of the markets without the worry of having to wire currencies around the globe to settle trades.

"As a hedge fund we have a cash settlement on every trade even if the trade is not going to settle for a couple of days. We are not limited to holding a position we can buy and sell as fast or as slow as we need, and the prime broker will net the proceeds of the transactions," said Taylor. "For us there is no physical settlement for currencies."

Unlike the stock market, trading currencies is a twenty-four hour a day job. And while Taylor and Williams do not physically sit in front of terminals all day waiting and watching the markets, they do have to take the timing of trades into account when they go home for the night or the weekend. "With all of our trades in all of our positions, we have established stop losses before we go home," he said. "If stuff is happening in the markets during times that we are not necessarily in the office, we will get in touch with the banks and transact business. There is always somebody we can call to get a trade done if we need them."

Overall the pair seems to be enjoying life as entrepreneurs, although like most start-up hedge fund managers, things have been harder than they thought. Prior to launching Cover, each worked at well-established firms: Taylor at Bank Julius Baer and Williams at HSBC, firms with large pools of assets and significant infrastructure to support their activities in the marketplace. Now that they are working on their own, however, they are finding that there are a lot of pieces to creating a successful puzzle. The hardest piece of the puzzle is, of course, raising assets.

Both Taylor and Williams believe that some of the push back that they have received from potential investors comes from the fact that the currency business went through a very difficult period in the middle of 2004. The markets for the most part during this time were flat or slightly negative or slightly positive. Simply put, it was extremely hard to make money in 2004. Taylor believes this caused many investors to turn away from the strategy. Their fund was up just under 7.25 percent for the year compared to the Barclays Currency Trader's Index, which was up just 1.84 percent and showed good investors that regardless of market conditions, they could make money. The index consists of an equal-weighted composite of managed programs that trade currency futures or cash forwards in the interbank market.

"Since we started, foreign exchange as an asset class has started to become something that people think of as essential to creating a diversified portfolio of hedge funds," said Williams. "And we believe that this is going to help us gain momentum and in turn help us raise assets."

Taylor and Williams are in it for the long run and believe that the hard part is over. Shortly, they will have a two-year track record and once that is established, they believe that they will gain the respect in the marketplace they deserve from investors.

Paul Reiferson and Jeff Lopatin— Americus Partners LP

When it comes to employing investment strategies there are those who try to reinvent the wheel every day and those who try to improve it. Paul Reiferson and Jeff Lopatin, who together manage Americus Partners LP, a long/short equity-oriented hedge fund in New York, prefer to improve on their strategy rather than reinvent it.

The two fall into the Ben Graham/Warren Buffett school of investing. They are singularly focused on building a portfolio that employs positions that represent a clear and defined *margin of safety*.

The idea behind Graham's concept of a margin of safety and one that Buffett has made a fortune employing, is simple: It is the price at which an investment can be bought with minimal downside risk. The caveat is, however, that the margin of safety price is not the same as the price that an investor calculates a share to be intrinsically worth.

Reiferson and Lopatin eat, drink, and sleep this relatively simple investment theory, and so far it has worked for them. Since inception in 2003, their fund was up 19.8 percent, net of fees, through the end of January 2005. They believe that building a margin of safety allowed them to create a portfolio that is relatively inexpensive compared to its actual worth.

margin of safety common stock issues are considered either under-priced or over-priced in the market relative to the intrinsic value of their companies. This brings error to truth for correction. To identify mispriced stocks, the value of a company is compared to its stock market price.

Lopatin and Reiferson met while working at Blavin & Company, a deep value, primarily long only, investment management firm. The firm is run by a Harvard Business School classmate of Reiferson's, Paul Blavin.

The Americus portfolio consists of long and short positions in debt and equity, all of which is united by a focus on capital preservation. All of the positions are built around the margin of safety. Reiferson says that the margin of safety is based on the recognition that if you lose 3 percent in order to get back to zero, you need to make more than 3 percent—but if you lose 50 percent, you need to be up more than 100 percent in order to get back to zero.

"NASDAQ investors suffered those kinds of losses when the tech bubble blew up," Reiferson said. "So our whole idea is to not lose money, not because it sounds good or feels good, but because mathematically it is a requirement because you just can't make up a significant loss."

To the two of them the margin of safety means that they are only investing in companies and, in turn, are constructing a portfolio of these stocks where a significant permanent capital loss is not at all probable based on asset protection, free cash flow, and the price paid for the company's share. The key is to buy companies that are cheap and represent a good value.

"If you were to ask somebody to look for change in any room most likely they would look under the seat cushions because that is where change most likely will fall," Reiferson said. "Well, value stocks seem to fall in certain crevices where you should always look. There are certain events like spin-offs, liquidations, and post bankruptcies—all dramatic events in a company that have taken the price down but the reason is such that you have to do research in order to understand it." So Reiferson and Lopatin look at every event to see if there is an opportunity to buy something cheap. When the companies come out, the two do research that digs deep into the story to see if it makes sense to add the name to its portfolio.

In their experience there are two reasons why a company would spin out a unit: (1) it is a dog and it is not fixable and (2) management is refocusing and they are spinning out something that is quite good but for some reason does not meet the strategic vision of the company. "Most subsidiaries when they are part of larger companies just don't get the attention or capital that they need and suffer from all the problems that you suffer from being part of a very large organization," said Reiferson. "But when they are spun out, many times they can make the changes that management of the subsidiary always wanted to do. A lot of times the accounting they are saddled with does not really reflect the reality of the new company's financial situation."

The idea is to gather as much research as possible in order to make the best and most informed decision about each and every investment opportunity. "We approach our research like any investigative reporter would approach a story," said Reiferson. "We look for employees, ex-employees, suppliers, and customers and build a relationship with them to create a dialogue with them to understand what is going on. We also look to build a relationship with the management team as well, to learn what we can from them."

For the most part, the fund will not invest in a company where they believe that there is a problem with the management. It comes down to a judgment call. "There have been situations where we begin to do our research and find that management has made misrepresentations to the press or in a filing that we have found to be completely false," Reiferson said. To them, this is a non-starter.

It is not hard to complete the research but rather it is hard to determine to which companies they should devote their time. Once they devote their time to something, they very rarely have a hard time finding someone to talk to or gather information from.

"When we devote ourselves to a company, both of us find and process as much information as possible on this company for a week," Reiferson said. "We can only do that so many times a year, so we need to be careful not to waste time on issues that are not worthy of the portfolio."

In order to be efficient, the pair uses a number of tools to screen for ideas. In addition to looking at event situations like post-bankruptcy and spin-offs, they also look for stocks that have hit new lows and new highs and stocks with the greatest percentage loss or gain. "There are situations when something happens with a stock and it may have a dramatic fall. When we do the research we find that the issue really does not matter so much and we can prove to ourselves that it is not a terminal issue," he said. "In those situations we then take a position in the stock when most people are avoiding it."

During the due diligence process, Reiferson and Lopatin really like to go onsite to visit a company to see firsthand its operation in action. It would be difficult for them to be comfortable amassing a large position in a stock if they did not see how the company functioned. "When we like a company once they pass a significant portion of our due diligence, we like to go and see them," said Reiferson. "There is no way that we could feel comfortable, backing up the truck (i.e., buying lots of shares) on a company we like in the face of a bad earnings release if we had not made a visit and met with management and learned what is going on."

Once the pair has amassed their research, they usually send a letter to management inquiring about a site visit. To date, the response to their inquiries has been positive. Reiferson said that his experience is that once a company knows who they are and what they have done and sees that they are serious, it is very rare for their request for a visit to be turned down. "They realize that it is worth their time," he said. "Sometimes, it feels like they are putting on a show for us, but for the most part we can actually learn something when we go out and meet with them."

Usually, they like to meet with the chief financial officer first and then with the chief executive officer because they seem to learn something from the CFO. Then when they meet with the CEO, they are all that much smarter about the company. When they go to companies it is rare that they meet with people that management does not want them to meet, but even in these contrived meetings the trips always seem to be worthwhile.

"It is especially worthwhile to go to see a manufacturing company," said Reiferson. "When you actually see the plant and walk on the plant floor and see how the products are made, you really get a better understanding of how the company operates."

And although it is important to get information from the company, it is also important to not always trust everything they hear from the company and to look for independent verification. "We gather all the information about the company then try to verify it with outside sources to determine if it is good," said Lopatin. "For example, if it is a manufacturing company in the healthcare industry, we call the group purchasing company to try to learn about purchase volumes and how well the product is being used."

Reiferson and Lopatin have come to appreciate that there are a lot of people sitting at desks who are experts at what they do and have nobody to talk to about it. So when Reiferson or Lopatin call, the person on the other end is not only interested in talking but is very excited about getting the call. "These people are waiting for someone to call and ask them questions and more importantly acknowledge their expertise," Reiferson said. "It is so counterintuitive but these people want to talk to you. Nine times out ten it is worth it to make the call."

Reiferson and Lopatin believe that this work gives them an edge over other funds that use similar strategies to manage funds. "Do we build the model, yes. Do we read every SEC filing, yes. Do we listen to every conference call, absolutely," said Lopatin. "But everyone does that and that just gets you smart enough to begin the process and see what questions to ask."

On average the fund has 10 long positions and 10 short positions and runs a net between 30 to 50 percent net long exposure. There is no specific target exposure because they have no specific view of the market. This allows them to test new investments by asking whether the position can achieve adequate returns without subjecting the portfolio to significant risk of permanent capital loss. They believe that if they did not subscribe to the idea of not trying to maintain a targeted market exposure then they would miss opportunities because they would be focused on their forecast rather than good companies.

"Every long in the portfolio needs to meet the margin of safety requirement and every short has to meet something analogous to the margin of safety requirement and the probability of loss has to be negligible," said Reiferson. "If you find great longs you put them in, and if you find great shorts you put them in, and if you don't then you don't. What is the point of targeting something? If you find something, it will naturally weight itself. So if the market goes down 90 percent, do you still want to be net long or market neutral? My guess is you probably want to be 100 percent long or 200 percent long depending on how you view leverage. The only way to self-adjust to opportunities is to not have a view and to not have a target."

To them finding a margin of safety is not debatable. The margin of safety comes down to building for a certain tolerance. The idea is simple: If you are going to build a bridge and you know that a two-ton truck is going to go over it, you build a bridge that can withstand a four-ton truck. You build for tolerance. "It is the only way to build a portfolio," he said. "When you look at something, you have to pay a price, say 60 to 70 cents on the dollar, so that you have the margin so that if something goes wrong you can't get hurt."

Reiferson and Lopatin do not see a day when their philosophy will change. After all, to them Graham's work, which came out more than 50 years ago, is timeless.

Guy Wyser-Pratte—Wyser-Pratte

Unlike other hedge fund managers who operate in obscurity and seem only to cater to their high-net-worth and institutional clients, Guy

Wyser-Pratte is truly a man of the people. His fund and the firm that bears his name specialize in risk arbitrage and corporate governance.

Wyser-Pratte has been working on Wall Street for more than 25 years and is often called the dean of the arbitrage community. In the past few years, however, his efforts to champion shareholder rights and to change many aspects of corporate governance strategies have won him many headlines as well as earning his investors superior returns.

"Our efforts to change the framework of corporate governance in the United States will destroy the 'just-say-no' defense that so many companies try to use when they are faced with a threat to their autonomy," he says. "It will end the abuses of *poison pill* and will force boards to think and act in the best interest of shareholders, something they often overlook.

poison pill any number of legal defensive tactics written into a corporate charter to fend off the advances of an unwanted suitor.

"People are fed up with the way management has been using poison pills. Instead of using them as tools to protect the company and its shareholders, management has been using poison pills as tools for entrenchment," he continued.

The poison pill was invented in the 1980s to give management significant control over the success or failure of a hostile takeover bid. Poison pills give shareholders the right to purchase hundreds of millions of dollars worth of shares very cheaply, which in turn often scares the suitor off because of the significantly increased number of shares needed to gain control.

Wyser-Pratte believes that instead of benefiting the shareholder, the use of poison pills often harms them, because bidders aware of the pills' existence will not attempt a takeover. This keeps shareholders from realizing the maximum value of their investment and allows management to keep power. Therefore, he has designed the "chewable poison pill."

He says, "Our pill keeps the best aspects of the conventional poison pill but at the same time it does not allow management to entrench themselves. It forces management to act in the best interests of shareholders at all times."

The first example of the chewable poison pill's use came in late 1997, when Union Pacific Resources Inc. withdrew its unfriendly bid to take over Pennzoil Corp. Union Pacific had offered $84 a share for Pennzoil, but the oil company threw up a just-say-no defense. The unsolicited bid offered a $20-a-share premium and would have added $1 billion to the company's market capitalization. Once Union Pacific pulled out, however, Wyser-Pratte stepped in, figuring that there was no basis for management's turning the deal away. By July 30, 1998, Pennzoil stock was trading in the low $40 range. In late 1997, the stock had been trading in the mid $60s.

Wyser-Pratte forced the company to act in the best interests of shareholders—he was one, since his fund owned over 1.5 percent of Pennzoil—by merging one of its units. It also has adopted a modified poison pill that gives shareholders a voice in future takeover offers. The chewable pill that Pennzoil adopted, based on Wyser-Pratte's efforts, says that if an unsolicited offer comes in at 35 percent over the average trading price, management must take it.

To make the board listen to his ideas, Wyser-Pratte launched a proxy fight, ran for a board seat, and filed a federal lawsuit to change a bylaw regarding board elections. Both sides in early 1998 reached a settlement that included Pennzoil's adding an outside director to its board and adopting a bylaw that gives shareholders the right to call a special meeting outside the annual meeting.

As part of the settlement, Wyser-Pratte dropped his lawsuit and his efforts to become a board member. Wyser-Pratte does not believe it will be the last time he will be able to get a company to adopt his chewable pill.

He has since moved on to fighting the poison pills and their protectors in general instead of in individual companies. As a Marine, he learned about fighting and more importantly about winning.

"This is going to be a battleground of major proportions between us and Delaware and all companies incorporated in Delaware, because we are going to take this and we are going to be actively assisted by the State of Wisconsin pension board and the Council of Institutional Investors," he says. "We want to have all companies whose poison pills expire next year adopt the same formula. Shareholders are fed up with the just-say-no defense because they have lost a lot of money."

Wyser-Pratte believes that his effort to change corporate governance is doing what is right by the shareholders. This sentiment is not often echoed in the hedge fund community. In most cases, hedge fund operators choose to do good things only after they have made their fortunes and can devote time to charitable organizations. Wyser-Pratte, however, makes it part of his everyday money management duties.

"When management hides behind their poison pill, they undo whatever amount of corporate democracy exists and make a mockery out of corporate governance," he argues.

He became interested in corporate governance issues when he was running Prudential Bache's arbitrage group. In 1974, he owned preferred stock in the sugar company Great Western United, but when the time came to receive his dividends, he realized something was amiss. Sugar prices were surging, but the checks never arrived. Finally, he and a colleague decided to sue the company for the dividends they were owed. Within a matter of days of the filing of the suit, a check arrived from the company and he realized that he could make money by becoming a shareholder activist.

Before 1974, he had been an arbitrageur. In its most simple definition, arbitrage is the buying of an article in one market and selling it in another. He learned the business of equity arbitrage from his father, who started the Wyser-Pratte firm in 1929 in Paris. It was subsequently merged into Bache & Co. and then into Prudential. In 1990, Wyser-Pratte resurrected the firm as a stand-alone entity—severing his ties with Prudential and operating the firm independently as his father had before him.

Wyser-Pratte usually works on three or four deals at a time, some in the United States and some in Europe.

"We try to focus on the best opportunities and work very hard at making them work for us instead of working on as many deals as possible," he says. "The way we determine what is worth doing is by looking at the amount of risk we have to take compared to the rate of return we expect from taking the risk. Something with a low return with a high risk is something we would avoid while something with a high return with low risk is something we would be very interested in working on."

Another situation that Wyser-Pratte was involved with was Taittinger S.A., the French hotel and champagne conglomerate, of which he and his partners control approximately 13 percent of the stock.

"We keep accumulating the stock and telling management that they have got to do what is right for shareholders. We are drawing attention to the undervalued assets in the company," he says. "Over there what we are doing is admired by the shareholder population, but the establishment hates our guts."

The fund's efforts to increase shareholder value in Taittinger S.A. were the subject of a front-page article in *The Wall Street Journal.*

Wyser-Pratte usually gets involved when a buyer walks away from a deal because the company has refused to accept the offer that is on the table. Once he gets involved, he works to make the deal happen. Although he does not talk to the suitor or have any kind of agreement with the company, his efforts are always focused on maximizing value for shareholders—which usually include him.

"In most cases when buyers walk away from a deal, they are expecting us to get involved, to run the company up a yardarm somewhere," he says. "Most suitors know that if we think the company is not acting in the best interest of the shareholder, we will turn our guns on them and make them maximize shareholder value."

There have been a number of times when Wyser-Pratte has heard of a situation and for whatever reason decided to get involved not by purchasing stock but strictly as an activist. Two cases of this were with the American International Group's attempt to buy American Bankers Insurance without letting others bid on it and Echlin Inc.'s attempt to get an antishareholder law passed in Connecticut. In both cases, his funds owned stock in the companies but Wyser-Pratte felt that he needed to take action to force the companies to look out for their shareholders.

"When you see that you can actually get things done by having the force of conviction to actually do something, that makes it fun," he says.

The firm's main fund at year-end 2004 had more than $150 million in assets under management and had a good year in 2003 and 2004, up 25 percent and 13.3 percent respectively.

Prior to launching the fund, Wyser-Pratte managed money at Prudential Bache. His performance record includes all of the years for which he managed money both in and outside of Prudential.

His firm operates out of lower Manhattan with 12 individuals. For the most part, he makes all investment decisions and works with colleagues to implement his strategies. Since the firm has been independent, Wyser-Pratte has done over 15 corporate governance deals, both in the United States and in Europe, and all have been successful. His investors are both high-net-worth individuals and pension funds.

Wyser-Pratte's efforts in corporate governance have come from paying close attention to what goes on in Europe.

"Our experience operating overseas has taught us how to work around a lot of the issues we are faced with here in the United States," he says. "Overseas, they don't have this nonsense. The key idea over there is to protect shareholders, not to entrench management. Here, because of the American Bar Association, the whole thing is to perpetuate litigation around the poison pill, and all they are doing is wasting shareholder money."

Although he has taken the lead on the takeover of such U.S. companies as Willamette Timber by Weyerhaeuser Corporation, these days he's focusing on Europe. Why turn your sights on a hotbed of government-sanctioned cronyism and old money—as in medieval old? Because the market punishes companies for poor management, making firms like Vivarte of France, Vendex of the Netherlands, and IWKA of Germany underpriced and therefore lucrative targets. "Corporate managers who consistently destroy value in a free market are replaced by good managers," he said.

But he acknowledges that he's found the going tougher on the other side of the pond. If European establishment interests have rendered corporations ripe for takeover, they've also insisted on putting up a fight. "There's more resistance on the part of establishment in Europe," he said. "In France, you have the old families who control a lot through double-voting rights. In Germany, it's the Socialist party that controls all the organs of justice. The company we're going after in Germany, not a single person on the board owns any stock. Not a single person in management owns any stock. What's wrong with this picture?"

To proceed, Wyser-Pratte builds what he refers to with a wink as a "coalition of the willing," a group of shareholders capable of pressuring companies and even governments into bending. In the end, whether they know it or not, the boards are forced to act in the companies' best interests. Vivarte (the former Group André), for instance, began, after the takeover in 2002, to show its first profits in years. "It's not just that you're trying to make money for people. As people have said about us over the years, we're on the side of the angels. We're trying to benefit everybody." Indeed, he added, much of Europe still needs to be taught what it means to have an equity culture. For this, Wyser-Pratte directly blames the rule of Communism, which evaporated from the continent only 15 years ago.

He doesn't believe that European companies aren't out to make a profit. Rather, he argues that European families and governments see their companies as personal and national property, rather than as belonging to the shareholders who bought it on the open market. The issue is particularly galling when boards attempt to hide behind national law in direct opposition to the fundamental contract of the European Union (EU) drawn up in Rome in 1957. Wyser-Pratte doesn't have any patience for tax havens like the state of Delaware that give a corporation's power over their shareholders in favor of what he calls "stakeholders." Similarly Holland, which Wyser-Pratte once referred to as a "banana republic in the world of corporate governance," has done its best to provide a shield for companies seeking to avoid the inevitable. Although he cheers on reformers like Charlie McGreevey, who became the EU's Financial Services Commissioner in November, he's realistic.

Still, things are beginning to open up. If Daimler could purchase Chrysler, why can't an American company buy the substantially underperforming Volkswagen? "What's good for the goose is good for the gander," he says. If the governments of Europe are reluctant to let "native" industries—think champagne in France, or Volkswagen in Germany—come under the control of outsiders, they'll eventually be even more hesitant to let them simply falter and go out of business.

What he'd most like, however, is for European corporations to embrace American-style business. "Stand up for yourselves," he says. "Create the values." Those who refuse, he envisions, will only stand in danger of ultimately bankrupting themselves. And as Taittinger, the great French champagne conglomerate that fought him in 2001, found out, even defeating Wyser-Pratte in the short term only opens the door to greater difficulties moving forward. When French courts blocked Wyser-Pratte's attempts at taking over Taittinger, he pulled out. But the company still found it necessary to restructure itself, incorporating much of what he had recommended.

Born in Vichy, France, in 1940, he moved to the United States with his family in 1947 and became a U.S. citizen in 1953. Wyser-Pratte was graduated from New York University with an MBA. The Marine Corps discharged him as a captain in 1966. He learned arbitrage from his father, Eugene Wyser-Pratte, who practiced the classical arbitrage strategy of buying stocks in one market and selling them in another.

"I did not find his business interesting at all," Wyser-Pratte recalls. "He explained to me that the business was getting more interesting and more intellectually challenging, so I decided to give it a look."

In 1967, his father decided to merge the family firm into Bache & Co. to have access to a larger pool of capital. He stayed with the firm until retiring in January 1971.

Guy Wyser-Pratte took over the unit and eventually came to run all of Prudential Bache's arbitrage activities. The situation got contentious in the late 1980s and early 1990s when Prudential was reeling from its limited partnership problems. When he was told that the firm had no more capital to use for proprietary trading because the securities firm's parent, Prudential Insurance Company of America, had shut it off, he decided to leave in 1991.

"In 1992, I did a lot of road shows and all I could raise was $3 million," he remembers. "But since then we have grown to our current size, and I think we are doing very well. There is nothing quite like running your own show and it is particularly helpful with all we do in corporate governance because we don't have to ask before we go after a company."

Asking proved to be a problem when he was working at Prudential Bache. Wyser-Pratte sued Houston Natural Gas because the board had turned down a bid and had prevented a subsequent bid from coming into the boardroom. He cleared the suit right to the top of Prudential after explaining that the firm's interests had been damaged. No one checked with the president, however, who happened to be in the office of the chairman of Houston Natural Gas at the minute the news flashed on the tape saying "Pru-Bache files suit against Houston Natural Gas."

"The chairman was about to sign a huge investment banking deal with Prudential and needless to say it did not get signed," he says. "Eventually, the chairman of Houston Natural Gas was fired for his actions and another firm emerged to take over the company."

Wyser-Pratte believes that his training in the Marine Corps is the most formative experience he has ever had and that it has played a significant part in his ability to succeed in business: "Being a Marine has helped me tremendously on Wall Street in building my career. It taught me how to size people up when I am in a situation where character is called on. You can judge pretty quickly who you can count on and who you can't when there is danger, and that skill is very important to being successful on Wall Street."

Although Wyser-Pratte has a lot of fun pursuing corporate governance situations, he is still very focused on exploiting arbitrage opportunities. As an arbitrageur, Wyser-Pratte gets involved with stocks when companies announce a deal. His method is to try to profit by capturing the spread between the price of the stock of the acquirer and that of the acquired.

"As long as we keep our discipline and do not go crazy in one situation while going about our business methodically we will be successful," he affirms.

Wyser-Pratte springs into action when a prospective deal is announced. Immediately following the announcement he and his team evaluate it and try to determine if it makes business sense. If they find that the risks and potential returns seem worthwhile, they invest.

Although corporate governance is where Wyser-Pratte gets all of the headlines, the firm still uses classical arbitrage strategies to post returns for its investors. He uses his risk arbitrage skills to determine the likelihood of the success of mergers and acquisitions, and usually when a deal takes place his firm has a position in the companies' stock.

"The key to being successful in this business is to continue to get better at what we are trying to do," he says. "We need to stay focused on strategies that we know will work and build our skills around those strategies."

In the Pennzoil situation, Wyser-Pratte was able to use both his corporate governance and his arbitrage skills to achieve a solid return. The oil company basically was fed up with fighting him and decided that the best solution would be to settle. As part of the settlement, the company agreed to his proposed bylaw and added an independent director to its board.

"It was a win-win situation for both of us," he says. "They were able to get what they wanted and I got what I wanted—and the shareholders were able to profit."

Wyser-Pratte believes that there are more important things in life than just lining both his and his investors' pockets.

"I am not involved with philanthropy in my business; my job is to make a decent return for investors," he says. "However, all of us in life look for some moral dimension in what we do, and I am able to fulfill that in what I do for a living."

Bill Michaelcheck— Mariner Investment Group

On Wall Street, there are stock guys and bond guys.

The stock guys can name all 30 Dow Jones Industrial Average stocks and at what level they opened and closed. The bond guys hang on Alan Greenspan and the Fed's every word and laugh when the popular press reminds their readers and viewers that yield moves in the opposite direction of price.

I am a bond guy. All of my formal Wall Street training was at a bond house and for awhile it was the way I made the bulk of my living.

So naturally, when I saw Bill Michaelcheck on one of the cable news channels talking about the Treasury market and his hedge fund, I became interested in learning more about him and his operation.

Michaelcheck is a bond guy. Since the early 1970s, after earning an MBA at Harvard, he has been trading Treasuries. He spent the early part of his career at J. F. Eckstein and Co. and the World Bank before finding a home at Bear, Stearns & Co. Inc., where he built the Wall Street powerhouse's bond department. Working alongside Wall Street legend Alan "Ace" Greenberg, Michaelcheck created a significant business at Bear, Stearns and, as a partner in the private firm that eventually went public, was rewarded handsomely.

In 1992, Michaelcheck launched Mariner Investment Group, a traditional hedge fund, in order to have a safe vehicle to manage his money. At the time we met in the late winter of 2005, the organization had around $7 billion under management.

"Over the past few years, our organization has evolved into what I would call a professional manager," he says. "That means we manage money in-house and that we also allocate money to other fund managers."

Mariner currently has a number of products that it uses to manage its partners' money. The firm's hedge fund is a low-risk vehicle that focuses on U.S. Treasury arbitrage and is managed completely in-house. It also offers a *fund of funds* that is a bit more aggressive that is managed through allocations to outside money managers.

fund of funds
an investment vehicle that invests in other hedge funds.

The firm also acts as the asset manager for an insurance company of which Michaelcheck is the chairman—a situation very similar to Warren Buffett's role at Berkshire Hathaway Inc.

"Today hedge funds fall into two categories. [The first category is] the large funds, which are really institutions, that have whole organizations and are really big companies," he says. "Then you have virtually nothing but a few billion-dollar guys, and then you hit the rest of us—people who have anywhere from $10 million to $500 million.

"What we want is to be a conduit for people to manage their money," he continues. "Look, if someone wanted to buy Robertson or Soros [type of manager], they don't need us; but if they wanted to buy the ocean of other people, which includes us, they better know what they are doing because they could really make mistakes."

Michaelcheck believes his organization will succeed because the needs of investors as well as the landscape of the industry have changed dramatically in the past five years.

"It used to be that there was some worldly guy who was a senior partner at some firm, who had $10 million in hedge fund investments with five different friends," he says. "Now you have big family offices and institutions that are putting out hundreds of millions of dollars in $10 million and $20 million chunks and they don't want to spread it around to guys sitting in their garage in Greenwich smoking cigars. It scares them, because if the manager blows up, the guy loses his job.

"So we are fashioning ourselves as an asset management firm that does hedge funds both internally and externally," he continues. "We are not consultants—we are hands-on managers who have been on the Street and understand that past performance is *not* an indication of future performance."

Michaelcheck thinks he is setting an example because, unlike others who have tried to build similar types of businesses, he and his colleagues were traders and are traders. They are in the markets daily and have been around the markets for a very long time.

"We have created a better mousetrap both internally and externally," he asserts. "We are not trying to be a personality cult. We want the business to be a business and we don't want our income hinging on the health of one of us."

Mariner evolved into its current form after Michaelcheck realized that there was an opportunity to provide to others the service that he needed for his own wealth.

"We are something like a fund of funds and we are a hedge fund," he says. "We are basically something completely unique in the world in which we operate."

At its offices in midtown Manhattan, the company trades fixed-income securities employing various arbitrage strategies in the Treasury and corporate bond markets. The firm also trades technology stocks using stock-versus-warrant arbitrage strategies to capture profits through market movements.

Mariner currently has a number of products that it uses to manage its partners' money. It operates traditional hedge funds—primarily in the credit and fixed-income markets—funds that offer investors low risk with steady moderate return streams and fund of funds. The fund of funds is invested in managers outside of the firm while all of its hedge funds are managed by internal managers.

"We have built a platform for institutional investors," said Michaelcheck. "By working with both proprietary managers and external managers we are able to deliver consistent returns to our clients."

In the spring of 2005, the firm moved the bulk of its operation to an office complex in Harrison, New York, about a 30-minute ride north of New York City. The idea is to put the bulk of its people under one roof in order to better serve the firm's investors and customers.

"It makes sense to move everybody to one location, it will make us more efficient," he said.

"We primarily run a low-risk hedge fund that takes advantage of price discrepancies in various fixed-income markets," he says. "We are not in this to get our adrenaline up; we are in this to make reasonable returns as risk free as we possibly can. By putting on lots of small trades that allow us to pick up a few basis points here and there, we are able to accomplish this goal."

The money the firm farms out goes to managers whose styles

range from high-yield arbitrage and takeover arbitrage to other arbitrage strategies. The difference between what the firm does itself and what it farms out is that the outside managers use "a little higher octane" than do the in-house handlers.

"Having come from the bond world, I do not have much faith in directional equity trading. While things appear to be easy right now, I have not found them to be easy and don't believe in it," he says. "I want to be able to understand what happens and what I think should happen, and do not want to rely on the Dow Jones Industrial Average. I don't need to hit home runs. I am happy employing strategies that have very little risk but allow me to pick up lots of nickels and dimes instead of occasionally picking up dollars."

Michaelcheck finds potential managers to invest with through word of mouth.

"People seem to know what we are doing and give us a call and tell us to check out this person or that person and we look and see if what they are doing fits our investment criteria," he says. "We don't care about how a fund ranks or rates on the various industry databases because it is not how we operate. We know a lot of people who know a lot of people who give us ideas."

The firm looks for fund managers who are employing arbitrage and other market-neutral strategies, as well as those using event-driven business strategies, like takeovers, divestitures, spin-offs, and bankruptcies, things that the managers can thoroughly understand and wrap their hands around. Once Michaelcheck determines which funds to invest in, he performs stress tests on the portfolio and tries to come up with a balanced portfolio of funds that can produce solid returns over various market conditions.

Michaelcheck believes that it is virtually impossible to pick stocks. If you look at all the mutual funds of the world and all their portfolio managers, he believes very few know what they are doing.

"There are always a few exceptions but statistically speaking you are more likely to find diamonds in a mound of coal," he says.

"Therefore, if no one can pick stocks, then no one can pick long and short stocks, and most hedge funds are throwing darts at a board.

"Everyone's stockbroker, every mutual fund manager, and almost every hedge fund manager claims to be the one person in the world who can pick stocks, and 99 percent of them cannot," he continues. "Being a hedge fund manager focused solely on stocks is a great marketing tool that is good for business, but for the most part the investors are getting the shaft."

Michaelcheck says that most of the hedge funds in today's marketplace do not add value to investors, and he believes that this is becoming more and more evident when the market moves sideways.

"If you look at the risk-adjusted returns of many hedge funds compared to those of the S&P or Treasuries, you find that very few categories of hedge funds have a positive alpha," he points out. "And most are just chugging along with the market. Chugging along with the market is not worth 1 percent plus 20," he says, alluding to hedge funds' usual management fees. "People are better off in index funds."

He continues, "Most of the hedge funds today earn money, good money, but they have a tremendous amount of volatility, and as such the investor would be better off leveraging up the S&P. But, if you look at what we do or others like us, we have volatility that is less than the five-year Treasury and are able to sustain reasonable growth no matter what the market situation."

"These are brilliant investment managers, but with all the ups and downs, the only guys making money are the hedge fund guys, because they are able to get 1 percent of total assets," he says. "Meanwhile, we are left waiting for them to do something for us."

Michaelcheck thinks that current market conditions are eerily similar to the situation 30 years ago when hedge funds took it on the chin and a number of funds blew up and went out of business.

"Right now, you can make a strong case that we are in the type of situation that we had in 1968. The market shot up, everyone on the Street started a hedge fund, and then a lot blew up," he says.

"My own opinion is that managers will not be able to keep posting the level of returns that investors have become accustomed to, and although we will not have a crash, many of the funds will go out of business because people are not going to pay for mediocre returns.

"Stock hedge funds are going to be the first to fall out of favor because managers will not be able to put up 20 percent returns without taking enormous amounts of risk," he continues. "Customers will pull money like they did in 1968 and the industry will take a number of steps backward."

Michaelcheck looks to the past to determine the future. For example the wake of the Russian default and the Asian crisis in the summer of 1998 put a real fear in U.S. bondholders that a recession was just around the corner. And although a recession did not necessarily materialize, the markets did spin out uncontrollably over the next few years because the fear—real or not—remained in the minds of investors.

"A lot of people lost a lot of money when Russia got killed," he says. "Many people needed to raise cash for liquidations or to meet margin calls, and to do this they had to sell positions in other stocks because all of the liquidity in the Russian and Asian markets had dried up. You could not sell Russian stocks or investments over there, and the only way to raise cash was to get out of securities that were doing well and had some liquidity. The situation is very similar to 1994 when the same thing happened."

Regardless of this situation, Michaelcheck believes that by employing hedging strategies and looking at risk-adjusted returns, he will be able to provide very good returns with very little risk.

"We do not move our money around," he says. "One of the good things about our position is that we have a steady stream of good ideas."

Michaelcheck got the idea of offering a fund of funds when a number of people he called up asked him what he was doing with his own money.

"I was interested in taking a somewhat more aggressive amount of risk with some of my personal money, so I started a fund of funds for that, and then slowly people heard about it and asked if they could get in," he says. "I do not market it. It is basically people saying, 'What are you doing with your money?' and one thing leads to another."

This fund had approximately $60 million when we met, in which Michaelcheck was the largest partner. He was finding it easy to raise money, but difficult to find places to put it.

"There is a lot out there and it is hard to choose good places to put the money," he said.

When he invests money on behalf of the insurance company, he uses a model similar to Buffett's, but instead of picking stocks he picks hedge funds.

"We pick the hedge funds and allocate the money to various managers to invest for us," he explains. "The idea is to be moderately aggressive and invest in uncorrelated funds so that we are always able to capture some returns no matter what happens in the market."

Although he believes that he is correct generally regarding the ability to pick stocks, he does not believe this judgment to be absolute, so he has some of the insurance company's money invested in stock funds.

"I could be wrong and realize that, so I have put some money into some stock funds to cover myself," he says. "My gut tells me that people cannot pick stocks and those that do are just lucky."

Besides the structure of his organization, also setting Michaelcheck apart from other hedge fund managers is that the firm does not always go for the jugular when it moves in and out of the market.

"Our trading strategy is not very glamorous: Our philosophy is to stay rich and not get richer," he says. "We like to sleep at night and enjoy other obligations. When we get nervous, we realize that we are not doing what we set out to do and quickly get back on track."

Nancy Havens-Hasty—
Havens Advisors LLC

Clearly Wall Street is a place where the old boys' network is very much alive and kicking. No matter how far we have come, it is still very hard for women to achieve the same prominence as men. Many women try and, for the sole reason of their gender, fail.

One woman who has managed to succeed is Nancy Havens-Hasty.

The fifty-something hedge fund manager, who has an MBA from Harvard and an undergraduate degree from Cornell, broke through the Wall Street boys' club in a very big way. Besides being the first woman elected to the Bear, Stearns & Co. Inc. board of directors, she is also considered by some to be the first woman investment banker ever to hit the Street. Now she is one of a handful of successful women hedge fund managers.

In 1995, she left the comfort of Bear, Stearns & Co. Inc.—one of Wall Street's powerhouse firms, where she managed more than 100 people, had responsibility for a trading account in excess of half a billion dollars, and was one of the company's 15 highest-paid employees—to start a hedge fund.

Her fund, Havens Partners, which had just over $250 million under management in the winter of 2005, specializes in risk arbitrage and distressed debt. With a team of eight, Havens-Hasty trades the debt and equity markets looking for unique opportunities that she can exploit for a profit.

Through the end of 2004, Havens Partners, the firm's domestic fund, was up 6.10 percent. A thousand dollars invested with the fund at inception in January 1996 would have been worth just over $3,300 at year-end 2004. Over the years Havens-Hasty has tried to build a team that complements each other, works well together, and most importantly, gets along with each other. "When you are working in a relatively small space, it is important that everyone gets along and can work well together," she said. "It is really a team effort."

Over the past few years, the firm has continued to jockey the line between merger arbitrage, distressed, and high yield. In late 1998, she moved out of distress because she could not find any opportunities—the pricing was all wrong. Havens-Hasty did not get back into distressed until late 2002 when the opportunities seemed to exist, moving some 30 percent of the firm's assets into distressed markets. By late 2003, she realized she needed to strengthen the team to help her cover the distressed side of the business, when the distressed part of the portfolio was up nearly 30 percent and the fund itself was just under 13 percent.

To strengthen the team, she brought in a former colleague, friend and investor David Feinman. Havens-Hasty has known Feinman for years and knew that he would be able to help her out on the distressed side of the portfolio and provide her with the ability to make money in the high-yield markets. Feinman joined the firm in February 2004 and has worked with Nancy to help take advantage of opportunities or "special situations" in the high-yield market—bonds that are of high quality although not the highest quality—but that nonetheless yield more than 10 percent.

"I left Bear, Stearns because I had gotten to a very narrow part of the pyramid and I knew that as a female I would not get any higher," she says. "I had got to where I got because I made money and I never had a losing year while I worked at the firm. When I got on the board, I suddenly found myself in a situation where it did not matter if you made money and it became 100 percent political, and I like making money more than playing politics."

Havens-Hasty, who is married and the mother of two children, believes that it would have taken an enormous amount of work and probably a change in her personality to move higher at Bear, Stearns, and she was not willing to do it. So she decided to leave and set up her own fund.

"I don't get my jollies from playing politics. I get my jollies from making money, and I realized that I should get myself into a situation where I could be happy full time," she says. "I enjoyed working within my own department and performing the research to get the job done but I did not enjoy the political aspects of the job."

Now Havens-Hasty works for herself and her partners to make money. Although she still has to deal with political/office issues like who the health-care coordinator or the network administrator is, it's all for her own benefit. One thing that has taken getting used to is that when there is an equipment problem she can't pick up the phone and see immediate results.

"When I was at Bear, if my machine went down or something stopped working, I could call the help desk and they knew because of my title and position that they had to help me right away," she says. "Now there is no one to call and when we finally do get in touch with something we are always at the bottom of the list. It takes a lot of getting used to, but over time I am sure it will be well worth it."

Her initial interest in risk arbitrage came after a stint as an equity analyst covering the computer industry.

"I was looking for something that would keep me interested," she says. "I had been an investment banker and covered stocks and got bored. Arbitrage was very interesting to me at the time and it has become something I love."

Today the fund specializes in risk arbitrage and distressed debt, but because of market conditions it has very minimal positions in distressed debt and has a focus on high-yield bonds.

"For the past year, distressed debt has been a pretty untenable place to be; default rates have been at an all-time low, and there were a lot of people who raised a lot of money when defaults were at an all-time high, and they were all chasing a tiny bit of merchandise—and the risk-reward was bad," she says.

While some of Havens-Hasty's contemporaries looked to

Indonesia and Korea for distressed debt deals, she says her research did not prove the investments worthy of her fund's capital.

"You don't buy Korea or Indonesia at 275 over," she says. "I would never buy those debt instruments because they don't honor contracts and you run the risk of ending up with nothing."

She did trade Latin America debt, in particular Brady bonds, when things got bad over there to take advantage of market opportunities. Brady bonds, named after former U.S. Treasury Secretary Nicholas Brady, are dollar-denominated international bank loans that have been converted into long-term debt instruments. Brady bonds, which are issued in U.S. dollars and are backed by U.S. Treasury zero coupon bonds, are used primarily by South American countries.

"When I don't know a market very well but it has totally fallen on its side, I will go in and buy the highest-quality instrument I can find and take the first 20 points out and let someone else have the next 30," she says. "That is the game I like. I am truly a vulture and I like it very much."

Since she has not been able to find distressed deals, Havens-Hasty has spent the bulk of her time doing garden-variety risk arbitrage. Her definition of that is going long the acquired company and shorting the requisite amount of the acquirer if it is a stock-for-stock deal. If it is a cash deal, she buys at the spread and works to protect herself should the deal fall through.

"In this type of market, it is very important to have the highest-quality deals you can find," she says. "If I think there is an enormous amount of downside I will buy puts to give up part of my upside to protect my downside. If the downside looks like a cliff, you don't want to be looking over the cliff without anything to hold onto."

The spreads are very narrow right now. In 2005, the time was ripe for deals, the Dow was down for the first few weeks of the year, the companies had lots of cash, and, more importantly, they had lots of stock. Havens-Hasty believed that there would be a series of big deals on the heels of the Gillette/Procter & Gamble deal and the

AT&T/SBC deal. She does not generally speculate on a deal prior to it getting into *The Wall Street Journal*. She simply waits for the deals to break and then tries to figure out how to trade them.

And although the firm focuses most of its attention on the U.S., it does sometimes look for opportunities in Europe and even Asia that may make sense to get into. "There has been a lot going on over in Europe," she said. "The difficulty in accessing these markets is information; you are in the wrong time zone, far away, and you don't necessarily speak the language."

One deal that worked out well for her was the Anheuser-Busch purchase of Harbin Brewery Group Limited, a leading producer of beer in China. The company was a $750 million company and although many people thought the deal was too expensive—it was trading at 19 times earnings—Havens-Hasty saw it as a great opportunity to make money. She believed that Anheuser-Busch was going to beat out the other suitor, Miller, because it was hell-bent on getting a significant foothold into the Chinese market. (Anheuser-Busch also owns a significant position in Tsingtao Brewery Co. Ltd.)

"It was easy to see how this deal was going to work and why it made sense," she said. "It was something that just made sense and while it was hard to get as much info as we would have liked on the deal and we had to keep the position small, we made a ton of money on the deal. It was an easy obvious thing."

As the market goes south, the deal flow is sure to dry up and when it does, Havens-Hasty plans on getting back into distressed situations.

"There will be lots of opportunities once the market shakes out," she predicts. "A lot of the distressed guys have been hit pretty bad because they have held on to their positions and now the competition in distressed is a whole lot less than it used to be."

To get information on deals, Havens-Hasty uses a combination of internal analysis and standard Wall Street research. Having worked closely with the Street for so long, she has established a network of sources of information.

"We like to get information from people who know things, not just people who are repeating things they have heard from someone they don't really know," she says. "Whenever it is possible, I like to get in touch with people who really know what is going on so that I can make the best decision. Whatever is the problem with the deal or the area most likely to cause concern, I will try to figure out who I know who might have some insight on it."

When she started out, Havens-Hasty found that she was too busy just getting the business going.

"It was amazing to me how hard it was to start this business and how many stupid details there are that need to be covered in order to get things up and running," she says.

"We were last on the list for things to get done for many of the companies we work with and that was a big change for me coming from Bear, where people knew that if I had a problem it needed to be fixed immediately and properly the first time," she says. "When you are not a member of the firm any longer, everyone else comes before you."

In the past year or so she has been able to break away from those tasks and do what she likes to do: research.

"I like doing the research and finding deals," she says. "It is important to understand what is going on in a particular situation in order to make sure you get the most out of it."

She also likes sticking to what she knows and understands.

"In order to be a good arbitrageur, you have to like to analyze a lot. It is like a game," she says. "It is about understanding the personalities and why the deal makes sense from a business standpoint as well as understanding what snakes are in the road between here and consummation. It is really a lot of fun because you are always learning something new and on the cusp of new technology."

Although she is constantly learning about new industries and companies, she does not believe in changing her strategy just to put up performance numbers. She thinks that when things start moving against her the best thing to do is to get out and wait for the market to turn.

"We will not have a position in our portfolio that is greater than 6 percent of our assets under management," she says. "I am not interested in taking unnecessary risks just to put up strong numbers. It is better to sit things out and wait for situations you understand than to go looking for things that you really don't understand and hope work out."

Havens-Hasty sees the most important part of her business as understanding how to manage risk and how to hedge to protect capital.

"Many people don't have any idea how to hedge or manage risk and therefore get into trouble," she says. "In order to be successful, you need to understand the instruments and how they trade, because if you don't, one deal can wipe out your whole business—especially if you are leveraged 11 to 1."

The main focus for her fund is to show strong results so she can continue to build the business.

"The best thing for us to do is to be ready for any direction in which the market would go," she says. "I think that we are on the brink of a real disaster, one in which the world goes into a major recession and takes us with them. The market could swing 400 points in either direction and we need to make sure we are prepared when and if that happens."

The fund ended up with a strong fourth quarter finishing the year up over six percent. Havens-Hasty said she was able to take advantage of what she called "a mediocre market" that allowed her to "load up" on lots of bargains and ride the wave as the market recovered.

Since late 2003, the firm has seen its assets grow significantly. Havens-Hasty plans on launching another fund later this year and expects that the firm will get to $500 million in assets under management relatively quickly.

"It was extremely painful to get from $50 million to $100 million but going from $100 million to $250 million was quite the opposite," she said. "We have gained respectability over the past few years, we have a five-year track record, our numbers are good, and people know us. It took a long time, but we have finally done it."

To that end, she believes that 2005 will be a good one, even though the fund was flat to slightly down in the first few weeks of the year.

"There is going to be a lot of opportunity in 2005. We are going to have to do a lot of work, but it will be worth it," she said.

Steps that Havens-Hasty has taken to alter her strategy include doing a lot fewer risky deals and taking much smaller positions as well as employing more shorts through the use of puts.

Havens-Hasty does not think of herself as an active investor but rather as a passive one. Although she specializes in risk arbitrage, her methods differ from those of Guy Wyser-Pratte, profiled earlier in this chapter.

For example, one of the big arbitrage situations in the past few years was the Pennzoil deal. Like Wyser-Pratte, Havens-Hasty traded the deal, but she got out at over $80 a share when the deal first broke and then shorted it at $69 when the deal started to unravel. Her mistake was that she covered her short too early.

"I covered at $60 a share and rode it to $37," she says. "Net-net Pennzoil has been good to me and I wish that it had been the only thing I had traded that year. I don't believe in make-your-own arbitrage. I much prefer to observe and analyze and sort of sit in the grass."

One of the rules she lives by is something that a good friend who is a hedge fund manager told her when she was starting the fund: "Never bet the business on one trade."

Steve Cohen—SAC Capital

Outside of Wall Street, nobody seems to know who Steve Cohen is. Although he has been the subject of a handful of articles, he is rarely quoted directly. He has been dubbed "The Most Powerful Trader on

Wall Street You've Never Heard Of" by *BusinessWeek* and called the best stock trader around.

Yet in the hedge fund world he is a giant. His company, SAC Capital, was managing just north of $8.6 billion in assets with more than 1,882 investment holdings, according to a 13F filing with the SEC made at the end of 2004. This is up considerably from when he was profiled in the first edition of this book in 2000. At that time, the firm had under $1 billion in assets under management. On any given day the firm trades nearly 20 million shares equalling nearly 3 percent of the daily volume on the New York Stock Exchange and nearly 1 percent of the volume on NASDAQ. It is estimated that the firm generates nearly $150 million in commissions a year to Wall Street brokers, making it a very important account.

Cohen is probably one of the best-known unknown hedge fund managers in the world. He started his business in 1992 after spending a number of years trading stocks and options at Gruntal & Co. Since then he has built a business that has never had a down year and has grown to be one of the hedge fund world's most sought-after investments. Although Cohen was trained by experience while working at Gruntal & Co., his formal trading education came at a very early age.

"I am a tape reader," he says. "I learned how to trade stocks by going into my local brokerage firm office when I was 13 and watching the tape. From there, I was able to determine what was going on, how things were trading, and most importantly how to see opportunities from numbers moving across the screen."

Today his fund organization consists of more than watching the tape. SAC Capital employs over 200 people, who range from traders and analysts to back-office support and clerical people. The fund, headquartered in Stamford, Connecticut, has an office in New York City.

Since inception, the fund has put up significant numbers—on average 40 percent per year. As Marcia Vickers said in her *Business-Week* article, his ability is "almost like turning water into vintage Bordeaux." Cohen and his partners are some of the largest investors in the fund. Their investment consists of more then 60 percent of the firm's assets under management. When it comes to performance Cohen and his traders are on the ball.

Cohen still believes that knowledge of situations and ideas is the key to success.

"This is an information business and the only way to be successful is to pay attention to what is going on and find situations that make sense," he says. "One of the reasons we do as well as we do is because we cover most of the sectors in the S&P and also have unique trading backgrounds.

"We do not get married to positions. If things are not working the way that we had hoped that they would, we get out," he continues. "We don't just sit there and let things happen; we are very active and always making trades according to what is going on in the market."

As SAC has increased its assets under management it has also been constantly evolving its trading strategies, styles, and techniques.

"The more capital you have to move around, the less you can move around as quickly, so consequently you have to develop a system that has a model that allows you to hold on to stocks even if the reasons why you went into the stocks have changed or your time frame has changed," says Cohen. "It is not a question of liquidity, because the markets are fairly liquid and we are in a lot of the big names. But the reality is as we have gotten bigger we need to have more reasons as to why we own something."

Cohen says that prior to opening SAC, when he was trading significantly smaller amounts of capital, he was able to buy 50,000 shares of IBM simply because he thought the market was going up. He based his decision solely on the tape and what he saw on the screen.

"I would make the decision to buy on the simple fact that I thought it was going up and I liked the way it looked without any fundamental reason as to why I liked IBM," he says. "Now we might buy IBM for a number of reasons. It might be that the computer sector is strong or that the analysts have expectations that things are going well. We now use different catalysts to make decisions as to whether we want to own something or sell something."

Cohen believes that one of the factors that has made his job harder is the explosive growth in the number of individual investors trading stocks—in particular those trading on the Internet. He believes that for the most part many of the investors trading electronically are momentum investors: When they see something go up, they buy it but don't have any real understanding of what is going on or why a stock's price is moving.

"My guess is that it is almost like a casino," he says. "The moves in stocks are larger and quicker than ever before and it seems like there is a bandwagon effect. When something is moving everyone wants to get on."

This has caused Cohen to adapt his trading style and pay closer attention to the price movements.

"If there is a piece of news out that I am going to discount because I don't think it is a big deal, normally I would go in and short the stock. But now I have to wait a little bit because things could get really crazy because there are so many other people involved in the game now," he says. "It is really unbelievable and I am going to make a fortune off of it."

An example of how Cohen has adapted his trading style and the changes in the game to his advantage is with a trade in USA Networks, Inc., and its then newly listed subsidiary, Ticketmaster Online—City Search, Inc. In the last days before the initial public offering (IPO) of Ticketmaster, USA Networks stock started moving up and Cohen decided to short the issue. His experience told him that in most cases when a parent spins out a subsidiary, the parent's price gets a big run-up and then when the IPO hits—boom!—the parent falls like a rock.

Although Cohen would not say at what price he went short or at what price he covered, prior to the IPO the stock traded as high as $32 a share and then fell to $28. His short position consisted of over half a million shares.

"This is an example of how the phenomena of individual

investors and Internet jockeys are causing the prices to move dramatically," he says. "USA Networks was discounted 12 times and the price still went higher because there is a lot of nonsense in the market right now. If the rules of the game had not been changed, this stock would never have gotten to be higher than $31 or $32.

"Nothing stays the same in this business," he continues. "You have to constantly adapt and evolve and learn what the new game is and then play accordingly."

SAC divides its capital into styles and sector portfolios run by various traders and fund managers. These styles surround a core trading strategy that Cohen runs with eight traders. He believes that having traders trade in groups allows the funds to be more profitable.

"I want people to be less worried about individual P&Ls [profits and losses] and more tuned into how the group is performing on the whole," he says. "For instance, if a guy has a bad day and is down a million bucks, the next day he is going to come in and not want to play the game. However, if the group account is up two million, he is going to come in the next day and still be in the game and will be trading. Maybe he had a bad day and did not score any points but maybe he had a few assists. We are trying a group approach, which over time will allow us to continue to perform extremely well."

Unlike other funds that charge fees of 1 percent plus 20 percent of profits, SAC has various fees based on the strategy or style the investor chooses. In some cases the fund charges as much as 50 percent of the profits without a management fee while other styles and strategies charge the standard 1-plus-20.

Cohen believes fees are justified by performance. He believes his funds have benefited from the carnage that laid waste to the industry.

"We benefit from volatility because we are opportunistic and when the markets get a little more volatile there are more opportunities to trade," he says.

While Cohen is constantly changing his trading strategies to adapt to market forces, he is also changing the structure of his company.

"I can see running as many as 10 different funds in the next few years," he says. "We want to be able to offer different strategies to meet the various needs of investors. Some people may want risk arbitrage while others want to invest in a specific sector. We are essentially going to create an organization that caters to whoever is interested in investing with us. I would call us a group of hedge funds under a single hedge fund roof."

Cohen, who was graduated from the University of Pennsylvania in 1977, got started on Wall Street in 1978 in Gruntal & Co.'s option arbitrage department after a friend of his brother's best friend got him the job.

"We basically would buy stock and hedge it with puts and calls," he says. "Back then it was a license to print money—everything was out of whack and it was really easy."

After a while, Cohen decided that hedging did not always make sense; he began to start holding on to positions and became a directional trader. When he first started trading at Gruntal he never spoke with anyone or used research reports; he made all his decisions based on what he saw on the screen.

"In the old days you could actually watch the tape and see what was going on," he says. "Now the tape moves too fast and there are more factors involved in trading and price movements."

Today, he is covered by all the major brokerages and is swamped with research reports and analyst recommendations. Still, he very rarely speaks with analysts or brokers and instead relies on his staff to handle the calls and countless pages of information.

"What we need to do is differentiate who is good and who is not and how to discount the investment banking aspect of the information that they are providing to us," he says. "When you get to know analysts over time, as the relationship grows, they will tell you things that can help you make a good decision."

Cohen hires both seasoned and unseasoned Wall Streeters to work at SAC. Lately, he has been hiring fund managers who could not make it on their own but who seem to thrive in the right environment—his.

"There are a lot of guys who try to run their own fund but have a hard time growing the business into something meaningful and end up nowhere," he observes. "Many of them realize that they would be much better suited in an organization where a lot of the stuff that they normally have to do is already taken care of.

"We have a few guys in our shop who were okay on their own, really nothing great, but who have just exploded since they have started working with us," he continues. "My guess is that there will be a shakeout in the industry when guys are not making any money, and I bet we will see a lot of guys who want to work with us."

Cohen is not sure how big he wants his fund operation to grow.

"I don't want to get big and put myself under a lot of pressure, but I would like to get big if it was managed the right way," he says. "In order to do that we would bring in talent and set up new funds, which would allow me to mitigate the risk and concentrate on what I know how to do without having to worry about how others are going to affect my performance."

As Cohen evolves his operation he adapts to the changes that affect all of Wall Street. One of the things that has really changed since he started in the business is the reliance on technology.

"It used to be you came in in the morning and you left at 4:30 and then you come in the next morning and you trade again," he says. "Now because of all the information that is out there, it has really become a 24-hour-a-day job. This job keeps going and going and going."

He says he isn't sure whether the change is good or bad but that the standard answer is that the job has become more interesting. The downside, of course, is that traders now have to sit in front of a computer all day and trading hours never end.

"This can be an all-consuming job but it is fun. Every day there is something new," he says. "It is a game. It's like playing a sport every day."

Hedge Fund Investing

When it comes down to it, there is no science to picking hedge funds or any investment, for that matter. For however many investors there are in hedge funds, there are at least as many different reasons why they picked that particular fund.

This chapter explains how various investors and consultants choose which hedge funds to invest in. Just as there are many different investment strategies managers employ to post returns, there are equally diverse ways to choose a hedge fund in which to invest. Hopefully, by reading this chapter you will gain a better understanding of how people choose managers, what to look for in a manager, and what to avoid.

Some people believe hedge fund investors throw darts at a list, while others believe investors perform hours of due diligence to determine which funds offer the right strategies, objectives, and management. Nobody really knows how people make their decisions, but one thing is sure: As Peter Lynch, the famed Fidelity Investments mutual fund manager, says, "People spend more money picking out the color of their refrigerator than they do on picking stocks." Lynch was talking about individual investors who do not have the wherewithal to perform due diligence on their investments and work off "tips." But the statement applies to sophisticated and unsophisticated investors alike. It was echoed by a number of people I talked to, including investors—both individuals and institutional.

One of the problems with investing in hedge funds is all the misinformation published by both insiders and outsiders.

"The press very rarely gets the story right," says one industry observer. "They lack the deeper understanding of what hedge funds are really all about. Another part of it is that hedge funds do not do a good job of communicating what they do to the press. The third reason is that editors would rather have juicer headlines than get the story right."

The problem seems to be that the press does not understand that there are many different types of hedge funds with various strategies and risk–return profiles. For the most part, the press writes about two or three different individuals and assumes that they represent everyone. The press seems to focus on master-of-the-universe activities and the whole concept of shadowy figures moving markets.

"Once people understand that not all hedge funds are Long-Term Capital or Soros, Robertson, and Steinhardt," says Ron Lake, a hedge fund consultant and fund of funds manager, "then they will be able to understand what unique and exciting opportunities exist and are available to investors."

This being the case, it is quite clear why people look to hedge fund consultants and investment advisers, as well as why many people in hedge funds don't necessarily know why they are in a specific fund or group of funds. Of course, one aspect of the funds, as with all investments, is greed. And one thing that comes with greed is hot money.

"A lot of people who invest in funds are doing so with hot money," says Steve Cohen. "These are people who put money with fund PDQ because it was up X percent last year and they believe it will do it again. However, as soon as the year-end comes and the fund does not meet expectations, boom, they pull their money and look to the next guy who is having or has had a good run."

Cohen says he believes most of the investors do not know why they get into specific funds. He feels that some of those who are not chasing hot managers are investing to feed egos or to keep up with the Joneses.

"People do very strange things when they invest," he says. "For the most part there is no rhyme or reason to their actions; they do it just to do it."

Cohen's sentiments are echoed by many of the consultants and analysts who help people choose fund managers and strategies. These consultants are investment advisers who specialize in the hedge fund world and for a fee will provide the investor access to their knowledge of the industry and its managers. As there are all types of investors, there are all types of advisers. Some work in conjunction with brokerage firms and hedge funds, acting as marketing agents for specific managers, while others work solely on behalf of the client and are paid a fee for their advice. For the most part, those who offer hedge fund consultant services do so on the up-and-up. Because the industry is so small relative to the mainstream investment world, it is not very easy to operate unethically or improperly for long. Still, investors need to beware of those who promise services that will lead to returns that are too good to be true.

Some of the most active hedge fund consultants are quoted in the popular press and interviewed on CNBC quite frequently. They are seen as able to provide an unadulterated view of the industry and of specific managers.

An Investment Adviser

Ron Lake and his brother, Rick Lake, run Lake Partners Inc. in Greenwich, Connecticut, an investment advisory firm that works with individuals, family offices, and institutions helping them with asset allocation, manager selection, and running their investment programs.[1] Lake is not like other hedge fund consultants because he does not market funds nor does he sell a database of information on the industry. In early 2005, the firm launched a fund of funds to invest in startup and new managers.

Because all the firm's clients differ quite a bit from one another, Lake can follow no specific guidelines to determine how to best meet clients' investment needs or to help them with investment decisions.

"We are basically investment staff for hire," Ron Lake says. "Someone may come to us and say 'I have a pile of money and I would like to know how to invest it,' while other clients may come to us and already have investments in place and ask us to help them with various aspects of their programs."

At the end of 2004, Lake was overseeing over $2 billion of assets. In some cases he has discretionary power and can pull the trigger on investments, while in other cases, the client pulls the trigger as he and his staff advise. The investor pays Lake's company a percentage of assets for his services.

Lake uses a number of different methods when deciding where to invest. The first step is always to determine what the money is for and what the client's investment objectives are.

"I think you have to approach hedge funds in the context of some broader investment game plan," he says. "Investors need to do this partly because it just makes sense and partly because there are so many different hedge funds with disparate risk profiles that you can use funds in many different ways either to augment returns or risk or to do both, depending on the investment program."

Lake believes that hedge fund investors are no different than other investors. Some are very clever and some are not; some stop to think about issues, while others do not.

"You need to understand the role you want hedge funds to play in your investment portfolio before you start talking about what kind of funds are appropriate," he says. "Once you establish what kinds of hedge funds are appropriate, you can then start talking about specific funds in which to invest."

According to Lake, some people hire his firm because they are looking to be educated, while others hire him because they want someone to bounce investment ideas off.

"There is no hard-and-fast rule or pattern to the motivation or behavior of the investor," he says. "This is partly because of the diversity of clients we work with, and also because some are very heavily involved in hedge funds and tend to be a more sophisticated investor and some are relatively new to it and tend to have a smaller allocation to it."

Once they determine the context for the investment (return objectives, liquidity, and risk tolerance are among other criteria), Lake determines what role hedge funds can play in the portfolio.

"If someone is a very conservative investor who has a lot of fixed-income assets with conventional equity investments, he or she might look to hedge funds as a way to get absolute returns from totally different areas," he says. "They may want a more aggressive piece, perhaps geared to macro managers—something totally different from anything else they are already investing in."

Lake says each client usually wants something different from his or her hedge fund investment. While the press may lump all hedge fund investors into a single category, he believes no two are alike.

"You may have two different types of investors who represent four different types of investment approaches based on what they want to accomplish," he says. "One can't build a house without building a foundation and as such we work very hard to understand the investment objectives in order to provide the right advice."

Lake's company typically plays a continuing role with clients, usually working with them for a number of years, establishing and building an investment program. Once investments are working the way clients want, Lake usually hands them the reins to handle on their own.

One of the big issues surrounding hedge fund investing is understanding what the potential conflicts of interest are between the investment adviser, broker, or third-party marketer and the fund manager.

"What bothers some people in the industry is when people wear two hats—one as a consultant, one as a marketer—and one is hidden under the other without full disclosure," he says. "With third-party marketers who are purely third-party marketers, things are simple—everyone knows that they are marketers—and consultants tend to be consultants; but there are a few that wear multiple hats. The problem only comes up when people don't make it clear where they are coming from."

Lake thinks that the hedge fund industry is really a bunch of different industries under one umbrella and that for the most part things are pretty stable in the hedge fund universe.

"The hedge fund industry is the same as the health care industry in that there are all kinds of people doing all kinds of things. At any one point in time, some parts are doing well while others are not—and sometimes at the expense of others," he says. "Right now there is a lot of concern among investors that certain hedge funds have failed to live up to their promise and are losing assets to withdrawals while other funds as a result are attracting more capital."

Over the years, the press has been quick to report that turmoil had taken over the industry and that investors were withdrawing capital from funds en masse. Lake believes that when it comes to hedge funds the press gets the story wrong.

"The press talks about how there are all these redemptions and all this turmoil but they missed the rest of story," he says. "The rest of the story is, yes, there are redemptions, but some of that money was being recycled to other funds and for the most part the capital was staying with alternative investments."

Lake believes that one of the biggest problems with understanding the hedge fund world is the lack of knowledge about its diversity.

"Some people seem to have a hard time understanding that there are hedge funds with all different styles and strategies and, like mutual funds, some will do well and others will not," he says. "Our job is to provide the customers with the right information to allow them to make an informed decision based on their investment needs."

To that end, Lake Partners has started to offer proprietary investment vehicles to new and existing clients. The firm currently offers two mutual fund wrap account products and in early 2005 launched a fund of hedge funds. The mutual fund products are unique in their investment style and strategy in that each of the products uses a specific group of mutual funds to find investment returns. The fund of funds is unique in that Lake is using the fund's assets to seed new, up-and-coming managers who he believes will do quite well in the years to come. All three of the products are being marketed directly by the firm to investors.

An Institutional Investor

For the most part, when one reads or hears about hedge fund investors, people think of rich individuals and wealthy families. Although these groups are very active in investing in hedge funds, institutional investors are by far the largest and most important user of such vehicles.

These pension funds, insurance companies, banks, brokerages, and national and multinational corporations represent hundreds of billions of dollars invested in everything from plain-vanilla stocks and bonds to exotic derivatives and hedge funds.

Most of the investors operate in strict secrecy. An unwritten rule forbids these investors and the funds to disclose who does and does not invest with specific funds.

"You will never get a fund to give up the name of an institutional investor because they represent too big an amount of investment dollars," says an industry observer.

To understand the process that institutional investors use to determine where and how much they will invest, one needs to get to the investment decision maker.

Unfortunately, most if not all institutional investors hesitate to explain their allocation and investment strategies on the record. One institutional investor who is very active in hedge funds agreed to be interviewed, but only if no names were used.

The pension fund is charged with managing $35 billion. At the end of 2004, it had allocated 15 percent of its assets to hedge funds. When we spoke in December, it was invested in 11 hedge funds, all of which manage their money internally and use long/short market-neutral strategies.

The institution's philosophy is to pursue investments at the forefront of the pension investment process to be able to make additional returns. It is willing to do things that other pension funds are not.

"If the others are not making the investment for a pure risk issue," says one of the pension fund's managing directors, "and if we think that is one of the primary reasons for not making the investment, we believe it will create extra returns for our portfolio."

The pension fund tries to control risk very tightly where its managers believe risk can become an issue. So, for example, it exercises very tight controls over its fixed-income program and moderate controls over its U.S. equity program.

"Exercising control allows us more latitude to take more risk with a long/short program or a higher-returning market-neutral and absolute-return strategies," explains one of the pension fund's managing directors.

"We have chosen the funds we are with because we believe that fundamentally they have unique insight and investment capacity and capability coupled with excellent risk controls," the managing director says. "Those three attributes are consistent throughout our entire investment program and we believe by applying them to hedge funds—which turns the dial up a little bit—we will be able to attain significant returns without adding significant risk."

The institution believes that investing in long/short strategies provides for a more efficient use of its capital. As such it plans on moving money from long-only managers who focus on matching the indexes to long/short managers who focus on individual stock selection.

"By changing our strategies we believe we are going to be able to leverage our managers' ability to add value and hopefully increase returns at the same time," the managing director says.

The pension fund allocates money by looking at the track record and diversification the hedge fund managers bring to the program. If they pass the review, the fund allocates between $50 million and $100 million to them.

"We will add managers as we add assets," the managing director says. "But we also realize that managers have a life span and some of our managers are decaying, so the trick for us is to determine when a manager has reached the top and then move on to another fund. Hopefully, we can get out of the fund before it hits bottom. The real test to the program is to not hold on to one fund too long."

The pension fund plans to drop one of its hedge funds in the next year and plans to add six additional hedge funds to its portfolio.

The pension fund limits its stake in a particular fund to 20 percent of its total assets. It believes that the best way to add value to its portfolio is to find young managers and grow with them.

"We are a big fund and it does not make sense for us to screw around with a $10 million dollar chunk," the managing director says. "We are looking for a manager that can grow into becoming a $2 billion fund, and if this is the case we may start with a $50 million position and grow with the fund to the point of allocating it $200 million to $300 million."

The pension fund doesn't use consultants to help pick hedge funds but its executives believe that as it expands, they may do so. They plan, for example, to hire a fund of funds manager to gain access to some hedge funds that it otherwise would not be able to invest in.

due diligence
questions by investors to the manager regarding investment style and strategy as well as the manager's background and track record.

"When it comes to investing in hedge funds, people are very conscious and cognizant of making sure *due diligence* is performed and the right choices are made," the managing director says. "We want to be very thorough and dig under the surface of the funds to make sure that we do not make a mistake and we realize that we cannot do it on our own.

"The advantage of hiring a fund of funds manager is that you can get into some funds where there is a smaller slice available—say a $10 million or $15 million piece," he continues. "Also, we can insulate ourselves from the risk perspective and we can blame them if things do not go well."

The pension fund will look for fund of funds managers the same way it looks for individual fund or money managers. It will choose a fund of funds that has a competitive edge, can be trusted, employs good risk control, and can share due diligence as well bring good funds to its portfolio.

"It is not simply a risk-versus-return issue with a fund of funds," the managing director says. "We are looking for a partner that can help us expand our use of hedge funds."

The managing director believes that many institutional investors make investment decisions based on historical attributes and the manager's reputation rather than looking ahead at how the manager could be expected to perform. While he believes this is a mistake for anyone, it can be a disaster with long/short hedge funds because it is a leveraged bet.

"There is a lot more risk associated with long/short investing than many believe," he says. "And you have a lot more riding on the manager's skill than with someone running a large-cap growth fund, so you have to be a lot more careful about picking this type of fund manager.

"I don't think many institutional investors are taking the extra level of thoughtfulness that is required with these types of investments," he continues. "Although one can never be sure what is going on in someone else's organization from appearances, this seems to be the case."

One of the nice things about having so much money is the pension fund's ability to be aggressive about pushing down fees, asking a lot of questions, and being really nosy about how the fund is being managed.

"Some people do not want to do business with us because they think we're too involved in the operation," the managing director says.

Some hedge fund managers' egos do not allow for pushy investors. One hedge fund in particular has not been willing to negotiate its fees because it believes it can replace the pension fund's dollars with someone else's in a heartbeat—and at a higher fee.

"We have not pulled the money out of this fund because we are greedy and we want the returns," the managing director says. "Just because they don't want us does not mean we do not want them. This is totally a game of egos and if we can put our ego aside then we are going to make more money than another plan sponsor who cannot put their ego aside."

The pension fund speaks with its hedge fund managers on a monthly or bimonthly basis and it reviews the funds' performances and positions daily. If a questionable situation arises, the pension fund managers are quick to call to find out what is going on.

"We are always sort of checking ourselves, saying this is what the market is doing, this is what we expect from a manager, and this manager is not acting in sync with the thought, so we need to understand why," the managing director says.

The pension fund's managers believe that now is the time to expand its exposure to hedge funds.

"There has been a lot of learning going on in the industry with other people's money and many investors have been scared away, and the opportunity is right to expand our program," the managing director says. "It is up to us to go in and pick people that we think will be the best going forward."

Third-Party Marketers

To be successful, hedge fund managers need only strong performance numbers and capital. Most people in the hedge fund world subscribe to the *Field of Dreams* theory: "If you build it, they will come" when it comes to raising money. If the fund performs well, investors will come. Still, building a track record takes a lot of work, and managing a hedge fund does not always provide for time for raising capital.

"It is one of the hardest parts of the job," says one fund manager. "When I started my fund, I knew I could pick stocks and put up good numbers but I had no idea how to raise money, nor was it a skill I was interested in learning."

As the hedge fund industry has grown so has the business of raising money for funds. Gone are the days of fund managers relying solely on family and friends for the bulk of the assets they manage. Sure, most funds start out that way, but once things get going, managers need to look outside their circle to the world of wealthy individuals, family offices, and institutional investors. To reach these people, many fund managers team up with third-party marketers. These firms specialize in raising money for funds. For the most part, they receive a fee for the assets they raise as well as a trailing fee for however long that capital and any new capital that their clients invest remains with the fund.

The world of potential investors is in reality much larger than it seems. As the stock market rallies, options are granted, companies are bought, and the economy stays strong, many more people and institutions become wealthy enough to meet the SEC's requirements needed to invest in hedge funds. Still, a hedge fund manager needs help in getting his or her story out, someone who has the databases and, more important, the relationships with investors.

Two people who do it are Linda Munn and Myriam Stephens. Together the pair runs Hedge Pros, a third-party marketing and consulting firm based in New York City. Hedge Pros was launched in 2002 when Munn and Stephens were introduced by mutual friends who thought they had a lot in common and would be able to work well together. "At that time, we realized that investors were looking for answers to the question, what do you do with your assets when the markets are going to hell in a hand basket and the only place you can go is cash," said Munn. "When we asked people where they were putting their money, the sophisticated investors all said the same thing—hedge funds."

It was clear from this simple amount of market research that hedge funds were the place to be and Munn and Stephens wanted to be involved.

Stephens had been working in the hedge funds since the late 1970s, first at a large fund and then at a number of investment firms developing prime brokerage services and administration functions.

"A lot of the things that people were now doing on computers, Myriam had done by hand, such as striking NAV and creating P&L's," said Munn. "And that skill set combined with my experience in marketing and sales at places like E F Hutton and Bear, Stearns seemed to be a natural fit for us to figure out a way for us to work together."

The idea was to come up with a real set of comprehensive services to hedge funds that includes everything from capital raising and client relations to helping them set up a business and running the operation.

"At first we went on a sort of fact-finding mission to see if the idea would fly," said Stephens. "We met with people that we knew in the hedge fund business to see what they thought of the concept in order to get an idea if it could work."

All of the people they went to seemed to be excited about the business. So the two wrote a business plan indicating how they were going to operate, who their customers would be, and where the revenue would come from. After a number of weeks working on the plan, they took it to a bank and received funding for their idea. "It was incredibly satisfying to go through that process and get a loan to start the business," said Munn. "It took us a lot of time and effort but it turned out well worth it."

The basic premise was that clients, in this case hedge fund managers, understood how to run a portfolio but did not have any idea how to run the actual business side of their operation. Initially they would help the managers with the business function of running the fund, and once the managers got to a point where they expended their friends and family and needed to look elsewhere for assets, Hedge Pros would be able to come in and help them raise capital. "We believed that once the managers went through their rolodexes and would need to go on beyond, they would need a new set of skills to not only present themselves properly but to also find investors and we could provide those services as well," Munn said.

Once the idea was hammered out, it took about a year to get the infrastructure in place, set up the business, and open the firm's doors. Hedge Pros officially launched in 2003. The business model was based on two streams of revenue—a project-based stream and an ongoing stream of recurring revenue.

"Hedge funds could hire us to do consulting type projects on a sort of one-off basis but once they hired us to raise capital for them, they would then pay us a traditional annuity stream of revenue," Munn said.

Traditionally in the third-party marketing business, the hedge fund manager pays the marketer a small retainer and then a piece of the fees generated by any of the investors the marketer introduces to the fund. For example, if the marketer introduces an investor who puts $10 million into the fund, the payout would be as follows: A standard hedge fund fee structure is a 1 percent management fee and 20 percent incentive fee. So if the manager was up 10 percent they would be paid 20 percent of $1 million in new profits or $200,000 and a 1 percent management fee of $100,000. The marketer would receive 20 percent of both fees or $40,000 of the incentive fee and $20,000 of the management fee.

"We were able to find both cash register ringing type of clients who ask us for product work as well as a number of longer term third-party marketing arrangements that together provide for a nice revenue stream," said Munn.

In their experience many fund managers have a hard time talking, walking, and in some cases dressing themselves, which together can present a real problem if the manager is trying to build a business and gain assets. Hedge Pros can help. They teach the managers how to make presentations and work with the managers to create a presentation and possibly advise them on how to act and approach investors.

"It is important to realize that an investor's time is very valuable," said Stephens. "We work with our clients to teach them to understand this and to teach them to not waste time when they are meeting with a potential investor."

Sometimes, the managers, while cognizant of the firm's expertise, find it hard to listen to their ideas or input. "There have been times when managers fight us tooth and nail about how we want to do something and the way they see it going, but finally they come around," Munn said.

Hedge Pros' clients run the gamut from new to established firms. Each has a different idea about what they want to do but all have the same wants—the desire for more assets under management.

"Managers who have been out on their own for a while and see that things aren't clicking are the ones who are the most receptive to our advice and guidance," said Munn. "They realize that they are going to have to change in order to really grow and they look to us to help them build a more successful business."

Although they are always looking for clients, in order for them to take on a new fund the manager has to meet certain requirements. Hedge Pros like to deal with managers that have at least a year or even 18 months of experience running the fund; they like them to have some assets, preferably more than $20 million; they have to be recommended to the firm; and, most importantly, Munn and Stephens have to like the managers. On average the firm works with three managers and focuses primarily on equity-based strategies that are sector funds.

"Look, the hardest thing in this industry is to raise money, but once you do raise some money it becomes a herd mentality," said Stephens. "So typically it takes one investor who leads the herd and then the rest follow. We knew this going in. That is why we chose to be very selective as to whom we raise money for and who we take on as clients."

Over the past few years, they have had to turn down as many potential clients as they have taken on for the simple reason that they can't get their arms around the fund's strategy. It is hard for entrepreneurs to leave revenue on the table when they are just getting started, but the pair believes these tough decisions make them successful and set them apart from other organizations in their industry. "There are lots of funds out there looking for money and trying to find new investors and we want them all to succeed but we realize that we cannot work with them all and that some of them are really not a good fit for us," said Munn. "It is better for both of us to say thanks but no thanks and part as friends than to take on an assignment that we are not going to be successful at or more importantly could hurt our business."

In their experience, the most important thing they have learned is the importance of performing due diligence on their clients and having the clients perform it on them before they begin working together. "Our business is about trust and relationships," said Stephens. "It is important that we can trust our clients and that they trust us."

Hedge Pros must be able to adapt to investors' needs and managers' wants. For the most part, managers want more money to manage, and most investors want to invest in specific styles or strategies based on market conditions. The key for Hedge Pros is to have the right products at the right time so that they can be successful and deliver good investors to their clients and good funds to their investors.

An Individual Investor

While institutions invest enormous amounts of money in hedge funds and represent the bulk of dollars in the industry today, individual investors also play a significant role. Most of the large funds tend to have a mix of institutional and individual money, while many of the smaller funds, those under $300 million in assets, usually consist solely of high-net-worth investors and family offices.

"When you start out, the first people you go to are friends and family and friends of your friends and family," says one hedge fund manager. "It is hard to attract an institutional audience and it is even harder to get them to invest in a new fund or even a relatively new fund with somewhat of a track record."

One manager told me that the bulk of the money that he used to launch his fund came from clients he had as a stockbroker at Lehman Brothers. "These people knew me, trusted me, and believed in my ability to pick stocks and make money," he says.

One individual who invests in hedge funds through a small family office is a doctor in Newport Beach, California. The doctor, who requested that his name not be published, told me his father had decided a number of years ago that the best way for the family to maintain its wealth would be to pool its resources into a family office.

"The family office allows us to take advantage of our belief in the efficient market theory," he says. "We believe that you need to look to alternative investments as potentially yielding a better rate of return with potentially the same if not lesser risk ratios."

The family office invests in a core group of funds that meet the needs of most of the family, while allowing individuals to invest in other funds, too. The idea is to make sure that everyone is provided for and that those who can tolerate risk do so and those who cannot do not. The doctor's mother, for example, who is 82, is in a core fund that all the family members invest in but she is also in a fixed-income fund with no one else in the family. Four nuclear families take part in the family office.

Over the years, the doctor has made some mistakes and has had to redeem out of a number of funds because they did not live up to his expectations. When a fund is not putting up the numbers he expects, he looks elsewhere for the returns. Currently they run five pools of assets: a core hedged equity portfolio, a PIPE portfolio, a commodities portfolio, a diversified equity portfolio, and a small fund of funds. Since they started managing their wealth this way, the portfolios have beaten the benchmarks but it has not been easy.

"We have had our ups and downs," he said. "It is very hard work and it is very labor intensive. Sometimes I wonder if I would have done just as well picking a fund of funds and letting them do all of the asset allocation."

In the core hedged equity portfolio, the doctor invests in mid-cap stocks. "Our mid-cap managers are not young guys that have not been around the block, and they invest very similarly to Warren Buffett. The fund consistently provides us with steady returns year after year. It is really a great fund for us," he says.

The doctor found the mid-cap stock managers after he decided that it was time to leave a private bank and look elsewhere for returns. "I basically ran spreadsheets on domestic equity managers and found that the fund was better than anybody else in performing in up and down markets," he says. "We found the other fund through a person we use as a sounding board for ideas who recommended it to us."

The doctor, who also acts as the managing partner without pay, does most of the research to find fund managers. He reads everything he can get his hands on and speaks to brokers, advisers, and investors around the country. "Finding hedge fund managers is sort of a networking kind of thing," he says. "I found one manager when I read about him in a *Barron's* article. I called him to schmooze with him and we have become friends."

The doctor also fields calls from third-party marketers and brokers who are paid to raise money for funds. The doctor says it does not bother him when these people call because they often provide him with information. "You have to evaluate everything for yourself and you surely cannot take their word for it, but there is really no harm in talking to them," he says. "These people don't make money from my end of the transaction."

The doctor does all his own due diligence and he recommends funds to the family, but each member makes his or her own decision. For example, his sister has chosen not to go into the new core fund. Instead she is looking for an investment that will provide her with a steady stream of cash rather than superior returns year after year.

As the managing partner, he evaluates everything from track records and previous employment to *Sharpe ratios*, risk–reward ratios, and *standard deviations*. He is self-taught and

Sharpe ratio
the ratio of return above the minimum acceptable return divided by the standard deviation. It provides information of the return per unit of dispersion risk.

standard deviation
a measure of the dispersion of a group of numerical values from the mean. It is calculated by taking the differences between each number in the group and the arithmetic average, squaring them to give the variance, summing them, and taking the square root.

learned almost everything he knows about finance from eight feet of financial books he keeps in his home. In some cases, he works with a few consultants and pays them a fee for investment advice.

"I keep extensive files and information on funds that we invest in currently and on those funds that we may invest with in the future," he says. "On average I probably spend less than four hours a week on following the funds. I spend more time worrying about individual stocks that I trade on my own than on how the funds are performing."

The doctor and his wife have invested in a fund that specializes in distressed securities, while the other family members have decided against it. "We chose to invest in a distressed fund because we believe it is a wiser thing to do than individual investments, because sometimes these things go belly-up," he says. "By being in the fund we are able to have 15 positions instead of three or four and are protected against the downturns."

The doctor runs the family office on a laptop computer that he uses to administer what he calls portfolios. These portfolios are either limited liability corporations or limited partnerships. Each of the portfolios, of which the family office has five, provides the members of the family access to specific funds.

"No one has ever gotten upset because an investment wasn't successful," he says. "What they do get upset about is when I don't get them performance figures as quickly as they think they should be made available."

For the most part, the doctor tends to stay away from the marquee names in the hedge fund world, instead looking for funds that he can grow with along with the manager.

"It is a small family office that allows us to invest tax efficiently and to find managers with good tax-efficient returns, in turn protecting and maintaining our wealth," he says. "We are not doing it for tax avoidance; we are doing it to make superior returns over time."

A Consulting Firm

When people ask what is the best investment bank on Wall Street, the answer is always Goldman Sachs Group. It is the premier investment house in the world and, whether or not people admit it, other houses want to be like it.

When it comes to hedge fund consultants the situation is very similar. One firm stands above the rest in terms of prestige and power: Boston-based Cambridge Associates. The firm, which was started in 1975, specializes in providing endowments and nonprofit organizations with investment and financial research and consulting and advisory services.

Cambridge Associates prides itself on being totally independent and a firm that works solely in the interest of its clients. It does not earn fees from financial institutions or money managers nor does it manage money.

"We are consultants in the true sense. We do not manage any money; we do not have a fund of funds; we strictly give investment advice and keep it objective," says a spokesperson. "We have no economic incentive to recommend one product over another."

The firm would not comment on its clients but they are believed to include 48 of the 50 biggest college endowments and many large foundations. One expert says the firm probably has over 700 clients investing in 500-plus hedge funds. The investments range from $1 million to $50 million and for the most part are spread between five and 10 funds.

Cambridge Associates does not market to colleges, but it does provide services through the use of sophisticated databases to help colleges see what their peers are up to.

"We give our clients investment advice and help them with asset allocation and manager selection," the spokesperson says. "Our biggest value-added is our research of alternative investments, both the nonmarketable side of the investment world, which are private equity and real estate, and the marketable alternative, which is hedge funds."

The firm keeps a list of hedge funds it likes and meets with about 10 hedge fund managers a week in its search of good investment vehicles. It gets between 30 and 40 calls a day from hedge funds looking to crack the institutional market.

"Any hedge fund that calls one of our clients is usually referred to us, and if we do nothing else, we act as a screen," says the spokesperson.

The first thing managers are told to do when they call is to send in material that details what the fund does and how it does it. Cambridge Associates picks through the stack of candidates and looks for funds that seem interesting. If, upon further review, the hedge fund is deemed interesting, the manager is invited to the office for an interview. About one in 10 of funds that call in is invited; one in 10 of those invited turns out to be a keeper.

"When they come in they give their presentation and we put them on film; we have them all on video," says the spokesperson. "If we like what we see, we really go deep. We will go visit them at least two or three times, we will get current and historical portfolios, and then we start digging from there."

The firm checks references, does SEC checks, and leaves no stone unturned before it recommends a hedge fund to one of its clients. "We look at whether a fund makes sense for a specific client on an isolated basis," the spokesperson says. "Usually the client provides us with a long list of criteria that the potential fund has to meet before we can recommend it to them.

"The universe of hedge funds ranges from unleveraged convertible arbitrage funds all the way up to the global macro players and every variation in between," the spokesperson adds. "So we are trying to make sure [the fund we recommend] fits with the clients' investment objectives and does what they are trying to do."

Cambridge Associates has found that many managers are willing to show them more than they show most other people because foundations and endowments are such fertile ground. The industry is inclined to believe that the money from these institutions stays longer than investments from offshore entities and funds of funds, which tend to move out faster. The theory is that institutional money may be harder to raise, but once it is in, it is in for good.

"We like to be early and if a manager has good background, a good resume, and, more important, a good strategy, we will look at them," the spokesperson says. "The key to a good strategy is to be in an inefficient area of the market because we do not pay for brilliance. Paying 1 and 20 percent to buy GE does not make a lot of sense, so we are trying to look for some inefficient area of the market where the manager can make some sense and can add value, long and short. It always boils down to if the guy is worth the fee, because most guys are not worth 1 and 20. It is a huge haircut for an investor to take."

Clients go to Cambridge Associates to receive advice on their entire investment program. The firm usually does everything from acting as a referee with the investment committee to making sure they keep the portfolio conflict free to developing and adding structure to the investment program.

"A lot of clients come to us who have 30 managers, ranging from cash managers to fixed-income hedge funds, equity hedge funds, and private equity funds and they look to us to add structure," says the spokesperson. "We probably got a hundred new clients last year; half of them had hedge funds and probably half of them did not know why they had hedge funds. We try to figure out what bets they are making because these things are called 'absolute return' or 'market neutral' vehicles and there really is no such thing."

Cambridge Associates believes 99 percent of hedge funds make directional market bets or what it calls in-directional bets. For example, some funds bet on liquidity and execute convergence trades, which are long something that is illiquid and short something that has liquidity. The fund is billed as one that can outperform its peers, regardless of market conditions, but when times like August 1998 come along and only liquidity counts, these types of trades blow up.

"In each case, we are trying to distill the strategy into what bets they are making and where the value-added comes from," the spokesperson says.

Cambridge Associates has some clients that have been investing in hedge funds since the days of A. W. Jones & Co. and Michael Steinhardt's first fund. Some of them are very sophisticated and have board members who run their own hedge funds or who have managed money professionally, while others have no money management experience.

"Sometimes the boards use us as a sounding board or they may come to us with an idea and we go run it down for them," says the spokesperson. "It really varies from client to client as to what they want from us and what we do for them."

The firm has also started building a client base with family offices, in particular those with over $1 billion in assets. Many of those clients need a lot of hand-holding and they come to the firm to get basic and completely original investment advice.

Cambridge Associates is paid either by the hour or as a percentage of assets. It does not earn any commission from fund managers.

"We have no discretion over any of the money," the spokesperson says, "so in the end all our clients come to us for the same thing: investment advice that they know is conflict free and completely objective."

A Manager of Managers

Although the rest of us eventually grow up and out of it, in the hedge fund world some people still like to hold their MOM's hand: that is, the hand of their manager of managers.

A manager of managers acts as an adviser to investors who are looking for a money manager but do not want to deal with the day-to-day responsibilities of managing those investments and do not want to go into individual hedge funds or a fund of funds.

A MOM will customize multimanager alternative investment strategies for institutional and high-net-worth investors. The strategies include the use of hedge funds, managed futures trades, and foreign exchange trades. Although MOMs have their fingers on the pulse of the markets, they do not try to time the markets. One of the benefits of using a MOM is that doing so provides the investors with both freedom and control over their investments—two characteristics that are rare in today's alternative investment world.

These organizations exert enormous amounts of control over the managers they invest with. The MOM usually requires the manager to sign a contract that details exactly what the manager can do with the money and provides for next-day redemption if the manager violates the contract. These organizations pick and choose individual money managers for their clients. The managers operate separate accounts for each investor. In most cases, an investor creates a portfolio of managers to handle all alternative investment needs.

One such MOM is a company called Parker Global Strategies LLC. Started by Virginia Parker in 1995, it currently has more than 15 employees in its headquarters in Stamford, Connecticut, has an office in Japan, and since its inception has advised on more than $1.75 billion.

"What makes us different from a fund of funds is that we are in control of what is going on with the money and the manager at all times," she says. "We tailor the contract with the manager according to what we are ready to do with the client's money. This means that we are always going to hire managers to run their strategy the way they typically run it. We don't want to ask them to do something they normally don't do or do something that may inversely impact their performance."

The contract that Parker signs with managers is very thorough. Not only does the contract describe the trading strategy in detail but it also includes limits on leverage, value-at-risk limits, and which instruments the manager is allowed to trade, as well as a list of those the manager is allowed to use as a counterparty. "If, for example, options are an integral part of someone's strategy, then they may be eligible to one manager but not to another manager with whom we allocate," she says.

Not all managers are willing to succumb to the controls Parker and other MOMs place on them. Those who do seem to make it all worthwhile. "There are more than enough very, very good managers out there, which means that we can provide some real value-added to our clients," she says. "The reason managers have been willing to do this is that they respect the work we are trying to do for our clients and look at us as a source of capital that provides them access to many different sources of funds through one entity."

Once a manager is chosen, Parker's company monitors trading activity daily. The firm independently marks to market every trade daily, unless it is something fairly illiquid, in which case the position is marked to market weekly. Parker also runs the positions through a risk monitoring system and monitors the activity to ensure that it is following the trading policy specified in the contract.

In some cases, the MOM knows more about the manager's portfolio than the manager does. For example, a manager who does not use value-at-risk or stress testing analysis may be able to learn something from Parker.

"It is not unusual on the risk side for our firm to know more than the manager on a quantitative basis," she says. "If managers do not know this information, it does not mean they are not good traders. All it means is that they probably did not work in a banking environment, at least not when those tools were becoming standard practices."

Parker likes to know what is going on with the manager. Although the firm is always looking for new managers, it primarily sticks with a core group of traders. Once she finds a manager she likes, she visits and asks the manager to complete a very detailed questionnaire. If Parker likes what she reads, the firm sends in a team of people to perform operational and risk management due diligence. The team looks at the manager's accounting practices, systems, and models, and checks references.

"Then we try to negotiate a contract with the manager," she says.

In 2005, Parker was tracking more than 2,000 managers both large and small in multiple investment styles and strategies in its proprietary database. It is not unusual for Parker and her staff to speak with the firm's clients and managers every day.

"We have a very high degree of comfort with most of our managers," she says. "Our philosophy is that once we find a good manager that still has capacity, we want to be the ones to use that capacity rather than just go try to find more and more managers."

In almost every instance Parker has the traders manage money for her clients in a separate account, but it has gone into a third-party fund a couple of times. Then the manager must meet specific requirements, including 100 percent transparency and next-day redemption capability.

Parker says that because of the amount of information and control she requires, there needs to be a lot of trust and a lot of both sides wanting to work together. "This is a relationship business, and we like to focus on relationships that are working well," she says.

In 2005, the firm was managing $500 million, a large portion of which was with managers. The firm did maintain a significant cash position to fund a guaranteed structure that it manages. For the most part, Parker's clients are banks and the customers of banks. The company manages the banks' own capital, while for their customers it creates private-label products that are marketed directly to institutions and corporations. The firm is paid both a management fee and a performance fee.

Parker also operates the first publicly registered and largest hedge fund in Japan. Marketed as a closed-end fund through IBJ Securities, it was started in March 1998 and requires a minimum investment of $1,000. Its shares do not trade in a public market.

When it comes to picking managers to work with, Parker likes to rely on word of mouth and her experience. She talks to people who allocate large sums of money, asking them whom they know, whom they see, and most important whom they like.

"I have never been able to find a manager in a database," she says. "In my experience having a database is the least important element in finding good managers."

Parker uses a network of large banks and insurance companies as well as people who have been in the industry for years to get information and ideas on managers. "There is a lot of camaraderie in the industry, and I think that a lot of people have a vested interest in giving each other tips on who is hot and who is not and try to help keep people out of trouble," she says. "There is a lot of very good information that is shared that is not readily available."

If Parker finds that a manager is not complying with the contract, she can end the relationship. Although it has never happened (most managers fix problems when they are told they are not in compliance), it is an aspect of the business that makes it unique in the alternative investment world.

The return clients receive ranges from 10 percent to 30 percent, depending on the strategy being used. Parker uses traders that employed strategies ranging from global macro and convertible arbitrage to U.S. and European stock long/short and managed futures.

Her company has stayed away from a number of strategies because of their risk, Parker says, explaining why the firm uses managers employing high-yield, emerging markets, and mortgage strategies.

"We do have a couple of managers that we like in high-yield and we were ready to allocate and decided not to this summer because of what was happening in the market," she says. "We are not quite ready to allocate to these strategies but do plan on going to them in the future."

Parker believes that being a manager of managers offers much more control than being a fund of funds operator. She says that she knows of a lot of smart fund of funds managers who found that a number of their managers were going to markets outside their normal routine and they wanted to redeem. These managers put in their redemption notices and by the time they could redeem the assets were gone—all lost.

"When you operate a fund of funds, you have no control," she says. "Even to be a fund of funds manager with 100 percent transparency, you don't have control if you can't get out, so what good does it do you?

"Our way allows us access to invest possibly with the same managers, but we are able to do it on our terms," she continues. "At the moment there are plenty of good managers that are willing to take money on our terms and therefore we have a business model that we like a lot."

Typically, Parker and her staff try to follow the market and get an understanding of what is going on, not in an effort to time the market but in an effort to stay out of trouble.

"Our views on the markets can cause us to have some small shifts in allocations but typically not huge, dramatic swings," she says. "Ultimately, the allocations are my call, but the principals here work together, talk, and share views, and usually we come up with a consensus on which we base our decision."

Parker believes in light of the carnage many hedge fund investors felt in the wake of the collapse of the equity markets over the last few years, people have now come to understand the value of risk management systems and in turn diversification.

"We have had a number of successful years when others did not," she says. "It was because we had the control, which meant that we had the capability not to be allocating in some places and very quickly shift allocations to a few managers who had good performance during those periods. Our control really made a huge difference."

Conclusion

Hedge funds have become a topic du jour as a result of the carnage that hit the equity markets in the early part of the millennium. It was an exciting time to be following the industry. For the first time in the twelve years I have been covering hedge funds, there was a real buzz about the industry beyond Wall Street's inner circles. Every day the phone would ring with stories of this fund losing money or that fund going out of business, while this fund had performed well and these people were getting set to raise some more capital. As Virginia Parker said of her business, the hedge fund world has a lot of camaraderie. Nobody ever wants to hear of a fund manager going out of business or someone who sustained enormous losses, even if they are vying for the same investors and in some cases the same investments. The industry is closely knit, from the accountants and lawyers to the prime brokers and the traders to the fund managers and the investors. The hedge fund world is a small part of Wall Street that has many, many more years of success ahead of it.

Unfortunately, the usual story about hedge funds shows something else: wealthy people investing with a secretive fund manager to earn enormous amounts of money and living lavishly and happily ever after. Every now and then there is a story about excesses like the helicopter to work or the 50 cars coupled with the huge shopping sprees. Recently, it has been the art and real estate purchases that have been making headlines. There are very few positive stories written about the hedge fund industry. There are even fewer to which the average person can relate. Instead the stories play on jealousy while exposing greed and making most people long for the wealth and privileged life that hedge fund investors and managers seem to have.

Well, here is a story with an entirely different spin that came out in the wake of the near collapse of LTCM. It is an oldie but a goodie.

On December 23, 1998, I had a message on my answering machine from Paul Wong, the Midas trader who runs Edgehill Capital in Old Greenwich, Connecticut. The message said, "Dan, call me—I have an interesting story to tell you." I figured that the story had to do with Long-Term Capital. Earlier in the day, the story broke that Meriwether and his partners stood to make a small fortune from their performance in the fourth quarter. I figured Wong was going to give me some color on the situation. I was completely wrong. When Wong and I finally spoke on December 24, he told me one of the greatest stories about hedge funds that I have ever heard.

In 1993, Wong got a call from the brother of a boyhood friend. The gentleman called Wong in desperation. It seemed that he had been doing some math and realized that the money he had been saving for his daughter's college education would be nowhere near what he needed. His brother suggested that he call Wong and ask for help. When the two spoke, Wong told the gentleman about the hedge fund he was starting and that he thought it would make sense for him to put his daughter's education money to work there. The father agreed, figuring that if Wong was putting his own money in the fund, it was as good a place as any for his money. He invested $45,000 as one of Edgehill's first investors. He had good years, like 1995 (up 134 percent) and 1996 (up 24 percent), and a bad year in 1997 (down 7 percent). Edgehill was up over 41 percent in 1998, and through the first six months of 1999 the fund was up 10 percent. The fund closed to investors in 2004 after not recovering from the tech bubble.

Throughout it all, the gentleman stayed with Wong. Toward the end of December 1998, Wong got a call from the father, explaining that he would need the money the following fall to pay his daughter's tuition at the University of New Hampshire. Although he was not surprised because he had been following the performance all along, he was quite happy. On December 24, 1998, his $45,000 had grown to over $125,000, enough to pay his daughter's college tuition and then some.

"Everyone thinks that hedge funds are about greed," says Wong. "In reality, hedge funds are about providing people with capital to do things that are important to them. What better reason to go to work every day than to know that the money you make is going to provide for a child's education?"

This story is not unique. There are many cases where fund managers and investors have used the proceeds of their investments to do great things. Two of the world's greatest philanthropists are George Soros and Michael Steinhardt, who combined give tens of millions of dollars away each year to help those less fortunate. Alfred Winslow Jones, the father of the industry, did not live a lavish life, but instead gave a lot of his money away, helping to make New York a better place to live. The list of hedge fund managers and investors who do good things with their wealth goes on and on.

Hedge funds do not destroy markets or ruin the economies of countries. They are simply private investment vehicles that seek significant returns regardless of market conditions. Managers are paid handsomely when they make those returns. It is a win-win situation for both investors and managers.

The problem comes when the managers step out-of-bounds and make mistakes. Then it is for the investor and the manager to determine how best to solve the problem. The idea of government influence, intervention, and regulation is not wise. It can only hurt the industry and its investors. The more government involvement, the worse things will be. Members of Congress, senators, and government regulators who have very little knowledge of money and markets should stay away from regulating the industry.

In a capitalist society, we subscribe to the theory that markets correct themselves when errors occur. If the market deems hedge funds too risky or too expensive or no longer valid investment choices, then the market will force a change. Until that day comes, the government and securities industry regulators need to keep out of the business and let the chips fall where they may.

Hedge Fund Strategies

The following list defines a number of hedge fund styles and strategies. The information was compiled by Nashville, Tennessee–based Van Hedge Fund Advisors, International, Inc.*

aggressive growth: Expected acceleration in growth of earnings per share. Often current earnings growth is high. Generally high P/E, low/no dividends. Usually small-cap or micro-cap stocks that are expected to experience very rapid growth.

distressed securities: Buying the equity or debt of companies that are in or are facing bankruptcy. Investor buys company securities at a low price and hopes that company will come out of bankruptcy and securities will appreciate.

emerging markets: Investing in the equity or debt of emerging markets. These countries tend to have high inflation and high, volatile growth. The definition of an emerging market is the market in any country with per capita GNP (gross national product) of U.S. $9,656 or less.

financial services: Manager invests at least 50 percent of portfolio in the securities of banks, thrifts, credit unions, savings and loans, insurance companies, and/or other financial institutions.

fund of funds: Manager invests in other money managers or pooled vehicles that may utilize a variety of investing styles, creating a diverse investment vehicle for investors. The manager may or may not choose to reveal to investors the funds in which he or she is invested.

health care: Manager invests at least 50 percent of portfolio in the securities of health-care products; pharmaceutical, biomedical, and medical services, and/or other health-care companies.

income: Investment with a focus on yield/current income rather than solely on capital gains and appreciation over time.

macro: A global or international manager who employs an opportunistic, top-down approach, following major changes in global economies and hoping to realize profits from significant shifts in global interest rates, important changes in countries' economic policies, and so on.

market neutral arbitrage: Manager focuses on obtaining returns with low or no correlation to the market. Manager buys different securities of the same issuer (e.g. common stock and convertibles) and works the spread between them. For example, within the same company the manager buys one form of security that he or she believes is undervalued and sells short another security of the same company.

market neutral securities hedging: Manager is long some securities and short others, with no real correlation between long and short plays. Presumably, net exposure to the market is reduced because if the market moves dramatically in one direction, longs might lose but shorts will gain and negate the move, and vice versa. If longs selected are undervalued and shorts overvalued, there should be net benefit.

market timing: Large commitments to one or two asset classes depending on economic or market outlook. Frequently, a portfolio will be invested 100 percent in either stocks, bonds, or cash equivalents. Anticipates/predicts timing of when to be in and out of markets.

media communications: Manager invests at least 50 percent of portfolio in the securities of companies involved in telecommunications, the media, publishing, information technology, the manufacture of cellular products, and/or other information services.

opportunistic: Manager changes from strategy to strategy as he or she deems appropriate. Can utilize one or many investing styles at a given time and is not restricted to any particular investment approach or asset class.

several strategies: Manager employs various specific, predetermined strategies in an effort to diversify approach, for example, using Value, Aggressive Growth, and Special Situations strategies in tandem to realize short- and long-term gains.

short selling: Strategy is based on finding overvalued companies and *selling* the shares of those companies. The investor does not own these shares, but is anticipating that the share price of the company will fall and borrows the shares from his or her broker. Ideally, when the share price does fall, the investor buys shares at the new, lower price and thus can replace, to the broker, the shares sold earlier, thus netting a gain. This strategy is also employed where the investor believes share price will fall due to company problems, and so on.

special situations: Usually event-driven. Manager takes a significant position in limited number of companies where situations are unusual in a possible variety of ways and offer opportunities: for example, depressed stock, an event in the offing, offering significant potential market interest (e.g., company is being merged with or acquired by another company), reorganizations, or bad news emerging which will temporarily depress stock (thus manager shorts stock).

technology: Manager invests at least 50 percent of portfolio in the securities of electronics companies, hardware and software producers, semiconductor manufacturers, computer service companies, biotechnology, and/or other companies dealing in high technology.

value: Manager invests in stocks that are perceived to be selling at a discount to their intrinsic or potential worth (i.e., undervalued), or in stocks that are out of favor with the market and are underfollowed by analysts. Manager believes that the share price of these stocks will increase as value of company is recognized by the market.

VAN U.S. HEDGE FUND INDEX¹: January 2005

	Jan-05	YTD 2005	2000	2001	2002	2003	2004	2000–2004 Net CAR²	2000–2004 Standard Dev.³
Market Neutral Group	**-0.1%**	**-0.1%**	**12.7%**	**7.8%**	**4.6%**	**14.2%**	**8.9%**	**9.6%**	**3.9%**
•Event-Driven	-0.1%	-0.1%	13.6%	5.2%	-1.6%	22.6%	14.2%	10.5%	6.8%
—Distressed Securities	0.4%	0.4%	2.1%	16.1%	1.9%	26.3%	19.9%	12.8%	6.9%
—Special Situations	-0.3%	-0.3%	18.2%	1.3%	-3.9%	21.0%	12.1%	9.3%	7.6%
•Market Neutral Arbitrage	-0.1%	-0.1%	11.5%	10.0%	8.5%	8.7%	4.6%	8.7%	2.7%
Long/Short Equity Group	**-1.4%**	**-1.4%**	**11.0%**	**4.1%**	**-4.0%**	**24.0%**	**9.0%**	**8.4%**	**11.7%**
•Aggressive Growth	-3.3%	-3.3%	-0.1%	-6.2%	-13.3%	28.0%	7.5%	2.3%	16.3%
•Market Neutral Securities Hedging	-0.4%	-0.4%	23.6%	11.8%	6.9%	6.2%	6.5%	10.8%	4.0%
•Opportunistic	-0.9%	-0.9%	14.9%	1.0%	-1.8%	28.5%	7.5%	9.5%	12.3%
•Value	-1.0%	-1.0%	13.3%	12.7%	-3.9%	25.2%	11.4%	11.3%	12.8%
Directional Trading Group	**-1.8%**	**-1.8%**	**14.5%**	**3.9%**	**6.8%**	**14.3%**	**7.6%**	**9.3%**	**7.6%**
•Macro	-0.7%	-0.7%	2.6%	2.1%	6.3%	19.5%	1.5%	6.2%	12.4%
•Market Timing	-0.2%	-0.2%	15.8%	3.7%	-9.7%	11.3%	3.8%	4.6%	10.7%
•Futures⁴	-2.4%	-2.4%	15.6%	4.3%	16.9%	13.2%	11.3%	12.2%	13.5%
Specialty Strategies Group	**1.1%**	**1.1%**	**13.2%**	**11.5%**	**9.0%**	**12.6%**	**7.1%**	**10.6%**	**3.3%**
•Emerging Markets	1.4%	1.4%	-3.2%	15.7%	11.2%	38.4%	19.0%	15.5%	13.3%
•Income	0.8%	0.8%	15.6%	10.8%	6.2%	11.4%	10.3%	10.8%	3.0%
•Multi-Strategy⁵	0.1%	0.1%	11.6%	8.3%	-13.8%	21.6%	4.9%	5.9%	10.3%
•Short Selling	3.0%	3.0%	23.9%	8.2%	32.1%	-22.6%	-8.9%	4.5%	25.4%
Van U.S. Hedge Fund Index⁴	**-0.6%**	**-0.6%**	**11.4%**	**5.8%**	**-0.4%**	**19.7%**	**8.4%**	**8.8%**	**8.0%**
Comparative Benchmarks									
S&P 500	-2.4%	-2.4%	-9.1%	-11.9%	-22.1%	28.7%	10.9%	-2.3%	18.5%
Lehman Brothers Aggregate Bond Index	0.6%	0.6%	11.6%	8.4%	10.3%	4.1%	4.3%	7.7%	3.7%

VAN GLOBAL HEDGE FUND INDEX[1]: January 2005

	Jan-05	YTD 2005	2000	2001	2002	2003	2004	2000–2004 Net CAR[2]	2000–2004 Standard Dev.[3]
Market Neutral Group	0.0%	0.0%	10.8%	9.0%	4.8%	13.1%	7.2%	8.9%	3.4%
•Event-Driven	-0.1%	-0.1%	10.1%	7.4%	-1.1%	22.5%	12.9%	10.1%	6.2%
—Distressed Securities	0.4%	0.4%	2.3%	15.1%	2.5%	27.4%	18.4%	12.7%	6.4%
—Special Situations	-0.3%	-0.3%	13.8%	4.3%	-3.9%	19.2%	10.4%	8.5%	6.7%
•Market Neutral Arbitrage	0.1%	0.1%	11.2%	9.9%	8.0%	8.4%	3.6%	8.2%	2.9%
—Convertible Arbitrage	-0.8%	-0.8%	17.0%	15.9%	10.0%	11.3%	1.0%	10.9%	5.2%
—Fixed Income Arbitrage	0.9%	0.9%	9.1%	10.6%	10.6%	9.0%	6.0%	9.1%	2.1%
—Merger Arbitrage	0.3%	0.3%	19.1%	3.7%	0.9%	4.6%	3.1%	6.1%	3.6%
—Statistical Arbitrage	1.1%	1.1%	38.2%	6.3%	9.2%	3.4%	3.2%	11.4%	8.1%
Long/Short Equity Group	-0.4%	-0.4%	9.5%	3.9%	-4.1%	21.7%	8.7%	7.6%	10.4%
•Aggressive Growth	-2.3%	-2.3%	-2.2%	-7.0%	-12.7%	27.1%	6.0%	1.4%	16.2%
•Market Neutral Securities Hedging	1.0%	1.0%	23.4%	7.7%	5.1%	7.1%	6.0%	9.7%	4.1%
•Opportunistic	-0.3%	-0.3%	13.3%	4.8%	-2.1%	24.4%	7.7%	9.3%	10.5%
•Value	-0.1%	-0.1%	11.6%	10.3%	-4.2%	23.4%	11.5%	10.2%	11.3%
Directional Trading Group	-2.1%	-2.1%	11.5%	4.9%	8.8%	14.3%	4.9%	8.8%	6.8%
•Macro	-0.1%	-0.1%	4.9%	1.7%	4.5%	16.5%	2.1%	5.8%	7.1%
•Market Timing	-0.2%	-0.2%	10.6%	4.3%	-4.4%	11.0%	3.1%	4.8%	8.3%
•Futures[4]	-3.2%	-3.2%	13.7%	6.5%	17.8%	14.2%	6.9%	11.7%	12.8%
Specialty Strategies Group	0.8%	0.8%	6.6%	13.0%	4.1%	20.5%	8.4%	10.4%	6.1%
•Emerging Markets	0.9%	0.9%	-8.6%	13.8%	-1.1%	41.3%	13.6%	10.5%	15.8%
•Income	0.8%	0.8%	9.1%	10.8%	7.9%	10.3%	8.8%	9.4%	3.1%
•Multi-Strategy[5]	-0.1%	-0.1%	10.5%	5.1%	-9.0%	17.7%	5.9%	5.7%	8.8%
•Short Selling	2.4%	2.4%	18.8%	12.0%	29.2%	-24.4%	-9.7%	3.2%	23.8%
Van Global Hedge Fund Index[4]	-0.1%	-0.1%	8.4%	6.3%	0.1%	18.6%	7.7%	8.0%	7.1%
Comparative Benchmarks									
S&P 500	-2.4%	-2.4%	-9.1%	-11.9%	-22.1%	28.7%	10.9%	-2.3%	18.5%
MSCI World Equity Index[6]	-2.3%	-2.3%	-14.0%	-17.8%	-21.1%	30.8%	12.8%	-3.8%	18.9%

VAN INTERNATIONAL HEDGE FUND INDEX[1]: January 2005

	Jan-05	YTD 2005	2000	2001	2002	2003	2004	2000–2004	
								Net CAR[2]	Standard Dev.[3]
Market Neutral Group	**0.1%**	**0.1%**	**8.6%**	**10.1%**	**5.1%**	**11.7%**	**5.7%**	**8.2%**	**3.1%**
•Event-Driven	-0.1%	-0.1%	4.5%	10.6%	-0.6%	21.4%	10.8%	9.1%	5.7%
—Distressed Securities	0.4%	0.4%	2.6%	14.1%	3.2%	28.2%	17.3%	12.7%	5.8%
—Special Situations	-0.4%	-0.4%	5.4%	9.0%	-3.6%	17.7%	7.7%	7.0%	6.3%
•Market Neutral Arbitrage	0.2%	0.2%	10.8%	10.0%	7.5%	7.9%	3.1%	7.8%	3.1%
Long/Short Equity Group	**0.6%**	**0.6%**	**7.0%**	**3.4%**	**-4.2%**	**19.0%**	**8.3%**	**6.4%**	**9.0%**
•Aggressive Growth	-1.1%	-1.1%	-4.7%	-8.7%	-11.4%	26.2%	3.7%	0.2%	16.6%
•Market Neutral Securities Hedging	1.7%	1.7%	23.7%	4.4%	2.5%	7.4%	5.5%	8.5%	5.2%
•Opportunistic	0.4%	0.4%	10.7%	9.4%	-2.3%	20.4%	7.8%	8.9%	8.8%
•Value	0.8%	0.8%	8.6%	5.9%	-5.4%	21.0%	11.1%	7.9%	9.2%
Directional Trading Group	**-2.3%**	**-2.3%**	**8.3%**	**5.8%**	**11.1%**	**13.9%**	**2.5%**	**8.2%**	**6.6%**
•Macro	0.2%	0.2%	6.2%	0.6%	3.8%	15.0%	1.9%	5.4%	5.2%
•Market Timing	-0.1%	-0.1%	2.5%	5.3%	3.0%	10.6%	1.5%	4.5%	5.8%
•Futures[4]	-3.8%	-3.8%	11.5%	8.8%	18.9%	14.6%	3.3%	11.3%	12.5%
Specialty Strategies Group	**0.5%**	**0.5%**	**1.2%**	**13.3%**	**1.5%**	**24.6%**	**9.5%**	**9.7%**	**8.8%**
•Emerging Markets	0.7%	0.7%	-10.1%	13.2%	-3.6%	42.2%	12.7%	9.5%	16.6%
•Income	0.8%	0.8%	2.6%	10.3%	10.1%	8.9%	7.4%	7.8%	5.1%
•Multi-Strategy[5]	-0.2%	-0.2%					6.5%		
•Short Selling	1.4%	1.4%	14.4%	15.8%	25.9%	-26.7%	-10.8%	1.7%	22.6%
Van International Hedge Fund Index[4]	**0.4%**	**0.4%**	**4.8%**	**7.2%**	**0.5%**	**17.3%**	**7.2%**	**7.2%**	**6.1%**
Comparative Benchmarks									
S&P 500	-2.4%	-2.4%	-9.1%	-11.9%	-22.1%	28.7%	10.9%	-2.3%	18.5%
Lehman Brothers Aggregate Bond Index	0.6%	0.6%	11.6%	8.4%	10.3%	4.1%	4.3%	7.7%	3.7%

©2005 by Van Hedge Fund Advisors International, LLC and/or its affiliates, Nashville, TN, USA (615) 377-2949. This Index is produced from VNMR's database of hedge funds, one of the world's largest collections of hedge funds. Historical Index returns are available at www.hedgefund.com. [1]Please see Explanatory Notes. The Van International Hedge Fund Index was formerly named the Van Offshore Hedge Fund Index. [2]CAR means Compound Annual Return. [3]Standard Dev means annualized Standard Deviation. [4]Unlike all other strategy Indices, funds in the Futures Index are not included in the overall Van International Hedge Fund Index. Beginning with the final August 2004 Index, funds of funds are no longer included in the Van International Hedge Fund Index. Historical returns for the Index were restated to exclude funds of funds. [5]Multi-Strategy was formerly named Several Strategies.

Glossary

accredited investor   an investor who meets the Securities and Exchange Commission guidelines required for investing in hedge funds.

arbitrage   a financial transaction involving simultaneous purchase in one market and sale in a different market.

bear market   prolonged period of falling prices.

bull market   prolonged period of rising prices.

derivatives   securities that take their values from another security.

due diligence   questions by investors to the manager regarding investment style and strategy as well as the manager's background and track record.

fund of funds   an investment vehicle that invests in other hedge funds.

leverage   means of enhancing return or value without increasing investment. Buying securities on margin is an example of leverage.

limited liability company   a legal structure that is the hedge fund investment vehicle.

limited partnership   a legal term used to describe the structure of most hedge funds and private investment vehicles.

long position   a transaction to purchase shares of a stock resulting in a net positive position.

management fee   fee paid to the manager for day-to-day operation of the hedge fund.

margin call   demand that an investor deposit enough money or securities to bring a margin account up to the minimum maintenance requirements.

margin of safety   common stock issues are considered either under-priced or over-priced in the market relative to the intrinsic value of their companies. This brings error to truth for correction. To identify mispriced stocks, the value of a company is compared to its stock market price.

offshore fund   an investment vehicle set up outside of the United States and is not available to U.S. citizens' taxable assets.

onshore fund   an investment vehicle that is set up in the United States that is available to U.S. citizens.

performance fee   fee paid to manager based on how well the investment strategy performs.

poison pill   any number of legal defensive tactics written into a corporate charter to fend off the advances of an unwanted suitor.

prime broker   service offered by major brokerage firms providing clearance, settlement, trading, and custody functions for hedge funds.

quantitative analysis   security analysis that uses objective statistical information to determine when to buy and sell securities.

Sharpe ratio   the ratio of return above the minimum acceptable return divided by the standard deviation. It provides information of the return per unit of dispersion risk.

short position   a transaction to sell shares of stock that the investor does not own.

standard deviation   a measure of the dispersion of a group of numerical values from the mean. It is calculated by taking the differences between each number in the group and the arithmetic average, squaring them to give the variance, summing them, and taking the square root.

Notes

Chapter 1   Hedge Fund Basics

1. *The Wall Street Journal* Staff, "Tiger Fund Has September Loss of $2.1 Billion," *The Wall Street Journal*, September 17, 1998, page C1.
2. These numbers were verified with Tiger Management's spokesman Fraser Seitel of Emerald Partners Communications Counselors on December 15, 1998.
3. The profit would be slightly less because there is some cost associated with the use of leverage.
4. Diana B. Henriques, "Fault Lines of Risk Appear As Market Hero Stumbles," *The New York Times*, September 27, 1998, pages 1 and 28.
5. This is the only firm to earn money on its investment. Many firms made a lot of money trading with Long-Term Capital as its broker.
6. Diana B. Henriques, "Fault Lines of Risk Appear As Market Hero Stumbles," *The New York Times*, September 27, 1998, pages 1 and 28.
7. Wyndham Robertson, "Hedge-Fund Miseries," *Fortune*, May 1971, page 269.
8. Ibid.
9. An accredited investor is defined by the Securities and Exchange Commission as an individual or couple that has earned $200,000 or $300,000 respectively in the past two years and will do so in the next year, or has a net worth of a million dollars. A superaccredited investor is a person and/or a family that has net investable assets in excess of $5 million.

10. Bethany McLean, "Everybody's Going Hedge Funds," *Fortune*, June 8, 1998, pages 177–184.

11. Ibid.

12. Reprinted from the March 1949 issue of *Fortune* by special permission; copyright 1949, Time Inc.

13. John Thackray, "Whatever Happened to the Hedge Funds?" *Institutional Investor*, May 1977, pages 70–73.

14. Carol J. Loomis, "Hard Times Come to the Hedge Funds," *Fortune*, January 1970, pages 100–103, 134–138.

Chapter 2   How Hedge Funds Operate

1. Carol J. Loomis, "Hard Times Come to Hedge Funds," *Fortune*, January 1970, pages 100–103, 134–138.

2. *The Wall Street Journal*, February 2, 1998.

3. Neither the Soros organization nor Mr. Niederhoffer would comment as to whether the funding came from the Soros organization. It is pure market and industry speculation.

4. Elsa Chambers, editor, and Sarah T. Fullilove, assistant editor, "1998 Prime Brokerage Survey," *Global Custodian*, Spring 1998.

5. It is the norm in the industry that the broker/marketer who brings investment dollars to the fund gets a piece of the fees that the dollars add to the fund's bottom line.

6. This comment is for illustration purposes only. It is not to imply that either fund manager farms money out to other managers.

7. James M. Clash, "Wretched Excess," *Forbes*, April 20, 1998, pages 478–480.

8. Michael Siconolfi, "Bond Market Still Punishes Hedge Fund and Investors," *The Wall Street Journal*, October 5, 1998, page C1.

9. Carol J. Loomis, "Hard Times Come to the Hedge Funds," *Fortune*, January 1970, pages 100–103, 134–138.

10. Ibid.

11. Stephanie Strom, "Top Manager to Close Shop on Hedge Funds," *The New York Times*, October 12, 1995, page D1.

12. Ibid.

13. I must make it clear that these numbers are used for illustration purposes only. It is impossible to confirm exactly how much money the Soros organization—or any other hedge fund for that matter—earns and receives for its efforts.

14. Most money managers meet and visit executives at companies they either are planning to invest in or already own.

15. *The Wall Street Journal* Staff, "Business Week Agrees to Settle Libel Suit Brought by Investor," *The Wall Street Journal*, December 18, 1997, page B6.

16. "A Hitchhiker's Guide to Hedge Funds," *Economist*, June 13, 1998, page 76.

17. Bob Davis, "Rubin Says Speculators Didn't Cause Asia Crisis," *The Wall Street Journal*, July 1, 1998, page A2.

18. International Monetary Fund Occasional Paper 166: "Hedge Funds and Financial Market Dynamics," May 1998.

19. Ibid.

20. Ibid.

Chapter 4   Hedge Fund Investing

1. Lake Partners Inc. also acts as a consultant to a fund of funds company called the Optima Group, helping with manager selection, monitoring managers, and structuring investment programs. At the time we spoke, Lake was not a marketing agent for Optima Group.

Index

Accountability, 5, 8
Accountants, role of, 2, 7, 57
Accredited investors, 4–5, 32
Administrators, role of, 2
Aggressive growth funds, 179
Alpha, 104, 128
American Bankers Insurance, 118
American International Group Inc., 20, 118
American-style business, 120
Americus Partners, LP, 108–113
Analyst recommendations, 143
Anheuser-Busch, 135
Arbitrage, 7, 16, 86, 116–117, 121–124,
    126–127, 132, 143, 180
Arbitrageur, 116, 136
Asian financial crisis, 9, 46, 85, 87, 129
Askin, David, 14
Asness, Cliff, 85
Asset allocation, 162
Asset classes, 107
Asset management firms, 124–125
Asset protection, 109
AT&T/SBC deal, 135
Attorneys, role of, 2, 7, 50
Audits, 95
Australian dollar, 106
A. W. Jones & Co., 26, 29, 38, 41, 47, 58,
    168

Bache & Co., 117, 121
Bacon, Louis Moore, 81
Balanced portfolio, 127
Bank Julius Baer, 106
Bank of America, 59–60
Bank of China, 23
Bankruptcies, 127
Barclays Currency Trader's Index, 107
Barron's, 163
Basics of hedge funds:
    current state of hedge fund industry,
        31–33
    historical perspective, 25–31

Jones, Alfred Winslow, 33–43
    Long-Term Capital Management, near collapse
        of, 13–25
Bear markets, 29, 46–47
Bear, Stearns & Co. Inc., 22–23, 124, 131–133,
    136, 157
Berkowitz, Howard, 80–81
Blavin, Paul, 109
Blavin & Company, 108–109
Bond arbitrage, 16
Bond market, 126
Brady, Nicholas, 134
Brady bonds, 134
British pound, 90–91, 105
Brokerage firms, 35, 59
Brokers, functions of, 7, 36–37, 50
Buffett, Warren, 20, 42, 108, 124, 130, 162
Bull markets, 24, 43, 47
Burch, Dale Jones, 38
Burch, Robert, 29, 31, 38–39, 41–42
BusinessWeek, 82–83, 139

Call options, 143
Cambridge Associates, 165–168
Canadian dollar, 106
Capital preservation, 4–5, 109, 137
Cash positions, 104
Cash settlement, 106
Cayne, James, 23
Central banks, 105
Chewable poison pill, 114–115
Chrysler, 21, 120
Clearing broker, functions of, 22
Clinton Group, The, 25
Cohen, Steve, 138–144, 146–147
Commissions, 61–62
Communism, effects of, 119
Company visits, 111–112
Confidentiality agreement, 65
Conflicts of interest, 149–150
Consultants/consulting firms, 7, 150, 165–168
Corporate governance, 114, 116, 118, 120–123

Corzine, John, 21
Cover Asset Management LLC, 102–108
Currencies, strength or weakness of, 104–105
Currency markets, 88–89, 91–92

Daimler, 120
Daiwa Securities, 60
Decision analysis, 99, 102, 140–141
Derivatives, 5, 7, 151
Distressed debt, 133–134
Distressed market, 132, 135
Distressed securities, 164, 179
Diversification, 173
Divestitures, 127
Doran, Barbara, 63
Dow Jones Industrial Average, 35, 85, 123, 127, 134
Down markets, 53–54
Drawdowns, 103
Druckenmiller, Stanley, 9–10, 82
Due diligence, 111, 145, 154, 160, 163, 171

Echlin Inc., 118
Economist, 87
Edgehill Capital, 176
EF Hutton, 157
Efficient markets, 105
Eichengreen, Barry, 90
Electronic trading, 141–142
Emerging markets, 172, 179–180
Equity arbitrage, 116
Equity hedge funds, 108–113, 167
Equity investments, 53, 149
Equity markets, 173
Euro, 105–106
European monetary system, 85–86, 91
European Union, 120
Event-driven situations, 181–182
Event-driven strategies, 127

Family offices, 161–164
"Fashion in Forecasting" (Jones), 33–35
Federal Reserve Bank of New York, 20–21
Federal Reserve System, 46, 86, 123
Fee(s), *see specific types of fees*
    structure, 2, 159
    types of, 29, 81–82
Feinman, David, 132
Fidelity Investments, 145
Fidelity Magellan mutual fund, 84
Financial crises, 85–87
Financial meltdowns, 45–46. *See also* Long-Term Capital Management; Tiger Management

Financial services, 180
Fine, Jerold, 80–81
Finger, Judy, 96–102
Fisher, Andrew, 85
Fixed-income assets, 149
Fixed-income hedge funds, 167
Fixed income indexes, 53
Fixed-income market, 126
Foreign currency options, 62
Foreign exchange (forex) market, 102–108
Fortune, 26, 28, 32–34, 36, 41, 47, 81
Free cash flow, 109
Fundamental analysis, 97–99, 103–104
Fund of funds, 124, 126, 129–130, 151, 162, 167, 180
Fund of funds manager, 153–154, 173

Gillette/Procter & Gamble deal, 134
Global macroeconomics, 103
Globalization for Youth, 39
Going long, 43
Goldman Sachs Group LP, 20–21, 25, 61, 63, 85, 88, 165
Government involvement, impact of, 177–178
Graham, Benjamin, 26, 41–42, 108, 113
Great Western United, 116
Greed, 15
Greenberg, Alan "Ace," 124
Greenspan, Alan, 123
Gruntal & Co., 139, 143
G-10, 104–105

Harbin Brewery Group Limited, 135
"Hard Times Come to the Hedge Funds" (Loomis), 28, 43, 47
Havens Advisors LLC, 131–138
Havens-Hasty, Nancy, 131–138
Havens Partners, 131
Haystack Capital LP, 96–102
Health care, 180
"Hedge Fund Heaven," 50
"Hedge Fund Miseries" (Robertson), 81
Hedge funds, generally:
    basics of, 9–43
    benefits of, 7–8
    common mistakes with, 8
    current state of industry, 31–33
    defined, 26–27
    fees, 29
    financial meltdowns and, 45–46
    historical perspectives, 1–3, 10–11, 25–31, 33–43
    impact of, 3

industry growth, 29–30, 47–48
industry reform, 24, 27
investing strategies, 145–174
  perceptions of, 3–4
  regulation of, 24, 27–28, 32
  research, importance of, 8
  risk factor, 4
  starting, 48–67
Hedge Pros, 157–161
Henry Street Settlement, 38
Herd mentality/psychology, 48, 89, 160
High-net-worth investors, 118, 161
High-water mark, 83–84
High-yield arbitrage, 127
High-yield bonds, 133
High-yield debt, 16–17
High-yield markets, 132, 172–173
Hot money, 8
Houston Natural Gas, 121–122
HSBC, 107

IBJ Securities, 172
IBM, 140
Illiquid markets, 16
Incentive fees, 159
Income, 180
In-directional bets, 167–168
Individual Investor, 28
Individual investors, 52, 141–142, 146,
    161–164
Indonesian debt, 134
Initial public offerings (IPOs), 1, 52, 141
Institutional Investor, 43, 51
Institutional investors, 31, 50, 89, 126,
    151–156
Internal Revenue Service (IRS), 32
International bond markets, 85–86
International Monetary Fund (IMF), 46,
    88–90
Internet stocks, initial public offerings
    (IPOs), 1
Investment adviser, 147–151
Investors, attraction strategies, 63–64
Italian lira, devaluation of, 91
IWKA, 119

Jacobson, Jon, 85
Japanese yen, 11, 105
J. F. Eckstein and Co., 124
Jones, Alfred Winslow, 6, 26, 32–43, 78–79,
    177
Jones, Anthony, 34, 36–41
Jones, Mary, 34–35

Jones, Tudor, 81
Jones model, 29–30, 36, 46–47
JWM Partners LLC, 25

"Kicking the tires," 49
Kissel, Lester, 40–41
Komansky, David, 22
Korean debt, 134

Lake, Rick, 147
Lake, Ron, 146–149
Lake Partners Inc., 147–151
Large-cap growth funds, 154
Large-cap stocks, 102
Latin American debt, 134
Lehman Brothers Holdings Inc., 60
Leverage, 6–7, 15, 17–18, 33–34, 42, 78–80,
    128, 154, 170
Levy, Leon, 80
Life, Liberty, and Property (Jones), 40
Limited liability company, 28, 32, 164
Limited partnership, 32, 36, 164
Liquidations, 109
Liquidity, 16, 97, 99, 129, 140, 149, 168
Liquid markets, 102
Litigation, 119
Long positions, 3–5, 27, 33, 43, 46, 112–113
Long stocks, 42
Long-Term Capital Management (LTCM):
  bailout of, 19–25, 86, 90
  historical performance, 18–19
  near collapse of, 13–25, 45, 176
  perceptions of, 3, 146
  regulations and, 86
Loomis, Carol, 28, 43, 47
Lopatin, Jeff, 108–113
Low yields, 16
Low-risk hedge funds, 126
Lynch, Peter, 145–146

McGreevey, Charlie, 120
McKinsey & Co., 23
McLean, Bethany, 33
Macroeconomics, 89
Macro hedge funds, 89–90, 180
Major, John, 91
Management, generally:
  accountability, 5, 8
  compensation, 7
  fees, 29, 128, 142, 155, 159, 171
  quality, 65–66, 110, 119
  style, types of, 6–8, 63, 126–127
Manager of managers (MOM), 168–174

Managers, profiles:
   Cohen, Steve, 138–144, 146–147
   Finger, Judy, 96–102
   Havens-Hasty, Nancy, 131–138
   Lopatin, Jeff, 108–113
   Michaelcheck, Bill, 123–131
   Reiferson, Paul, 108–113
   Taylor, David, 102–108
   Topkis, Doug, 96–102
   Williams, Mike, 102–108
   Wyser-Pratte, Guy, 113–123
Margin calls, 13
Margin of safety, 108–109, 113
Mariner Investment Group, 123–131
Market conditions, 128–129, 133
Market-neutral strategies, 127, 167, 180–181
Market swings, 42
Market timing, 181
Market volatility, 11
Marron, Donald, 23
Maverick Capital, 25
Media, impact of, 27, 45, 66, 82, 85–90, 146,
     150, 175–176, 181
Merger arbitrage, 132
Meriwether, John, 14–20, 24–25
Merrill Lynch & Co. Inc., 21–23, 60
Merton, Robert, 14
Mexican peso, 105–106
Michaelcheck, Bill, 50, 123–131
Micro-cap stocks, 57
Mid-cap stock, 162
Midas traders, 2, 79–80, 84, 87, 176
Miller (brewery), 135
Misinformation, 146
Mispriced opportunities, 97
Momentum investors, 141
Morgan, J. P., 20
Morgan Stanley, 25
Mortgage strategies, 172
Moving average, 103
MSCI World Equity Index 100, 53–54
Mullins, David, 14
Munn, Linda, 157–158, 160
Mutual funds:
   characteristics of, 150–151
   hedge funds distinguished from, 4–5
   regulation of, 31
   timing scandal, 86

NASDAQ, 139
Nash, Jack, 50–51, 80
Natural Health Trends Corp., 101
Nelson, Daniel, 40

Net asset value (NAV), 157
Neuberger, Roy, 26, 37, 40
Neuberger Berman Inc., 26, 36, 39
New York Stock Exchange (NYSE), 13, 47, 139
New York Times, 42, 81
New Zealand dollar, 106
Niederhoffer, Victor, 14, 55–56

Odyssey Parters, 50, 80
Operation(s), *see specific funds*
   economic influences, generally, 86–90
   industry patriarchs, 80–85
   leverage, 78–80
   media perspectives, 85–90
   regulations, 67–78
   starting a hedge fund, 48–67
Opportunistic strategy, 181
Option arbitrage, 143
Options, 104, 170

PaineWebber Group Inc., 23
Parker, Virginia, 169–175
Parker Global Strategies LLC, 169–173
Parlux Fragrances Inc., 100–101
Partnership agreement, 83
Passive investor, 138
Patriarchs, 80–85
Pennzoil Corp., 115, 123, 138
Pension fund management, 118, 152–156
Performance fee, 29, 171
Philanthropy, 38, 81
Plain-vanilla stocks, 151
Poison pill, 114–116, 119
Portfolio diversification, 5, 8, 162
Postbankruptcies, 109, 111
Prime brokers, role of, 2, 51–52, 57–63
Private equity investments, 166–167
Private investment partnerships, 85
Profits and losses (P&Ls), 142, 157
Proxy fights, 115
Prudent investors, 48
Prudential Bache, 116–117, 121–122
Prudential Insurance Company of America, 121
Put options, 143

Quantitative analysis, 14–15
Quantum Fund, 9–10, 82

Real estate investments, 166
Recession, 129, 137
Redemption notices, 173
Registered Investment Advisor, 32
Regulations, 4–5, 67–68

Reiferson, Paul, 108–113
Reporting requirements, 31
Research, importance of, 8, 104, 110–112,
 134–136, 163–164, 166
Return(s):
 absolute, 167
 objectives, 149
 rate of, 52
Risk:
 arbitrage, 7, 114, 122, 133–134, 138, 143
 exposure, 62
 impact of, 15
 management, 101, 137–138, 152, 171, 173
 minimization, 27
 mitigation, 143
 profiles, 148
 tolerance, 149
Risk/return analysis, 117, 154
Risk-reward analysis, 99, 163
Robertson, Julian, 6, 11–12, 30–31, 65, 67,
 81–83, 125, 146
Robertson, Wyndham, 81
Rogers, Jim, 32, 53–55
Rubin, Robert, 88
Russia, financial crisis in, 9–11, 46, 87, 129

SAC Capital, 25, 138–144
Salomon Brothers, 16–17, 25, 64, 85
Scholes, Myron, 14
Sector funds, 160
Sector portfolios, 142
Securities analysis, 26
Securities and Exchange Commission (SEC), 4–5,
 27–28, 31–32, 42–43, 46, 80–81, 86, 157,
 166
Shareholder value, 117–118
Sharpe ratio, 163
Short positions, 3–5, 27, 33, 47, 79, 106,
 112–113, 138
Short selling, 42–43, 181
Sideways market, 128
Site visits, 111–112
Slater, Robert, 91
Slippage, 64–65
Small-cap equities, 63
Soros, George, 3, 6, 11, 20, 51, 53, 56, 65, 81,
 87–88, 90–92, 125, 146, 177
Soros, Jonathon, 51
Soros, Robert, 51
Soros: The Life, Times, and Trading Secrets of the
 World's Greatest Investor (Slater), 91
Soros Fund Management, 51, 88
South African rand, 105

Special situations, 181–182
Spector, Warren, 23
Speculation/speculators, 88, 105, 135
Spin-offs, 109–111, 127
Spot trading, 106
Stakeholders, 120
Standard & Poor's 500 (S&P 500), 52–54,
 96
Standard deviation, 163
Starting a hedge fund:
 administrative costs, 58
 attracting investors, 63–64
 capital needs, 48–49, 58
 ease of entry, 53, 55–57, 60–61
 home offices, 49–50
 industry growth, 52, 62
 information sources, 49
 management quality, 65–66
 minimum investment requirements, 67
 opening accounts, 61–62
 prime brokers, 51–52, 57–63
 referrals, 51
 trends in, 64–67
Steinhardt, Michael, 6, 43, 50–51, 55, 80–81,
 83–84, 146, 168, 177
Steinhardt Fine Berkowitz & Co., 43
Stephens, Myriam, 157, 159–160
Stock-for-stock deal, 134
Stock hedge funds, 129
Stock market crash, 60
Stock options, 52
Stock selection, 127–128, 130, 145, 153,
 156
Stop losses, 106
Stress testing analysis, 170
Strong, Richard, 86
Strong Funds, 86
Subsidiaries, 110
Super hedge funds, 81
Swiss franc, 105

Taittinger S.A., 117, 120
Takeover arbitrage, 127
Takeover targets, 118–119
Taylor, David, 102–108
Technical analysis, 103
Technical indicators, 97–99, 104
Technology bubble, 1–2, 46
Technology stocks, 30, 182
Thai baht, 85, 88–89, 105
Third-party marketers, 63, 95, 150, 156–161
Ticketmaster Online–City Search, Inc., 141
Tiger Management, 11–12, 30–31

Topkis, Doug, 96–102
Trading desks, 14, 59
Tsingtao Brewery Co. Ltd., 135

Ulysses fund, 50–51
Union Pacific Resources Inc., 115
U.S. dollar, 105
U.S. Treasuries, 16, 102, 123–124, 126, 128,
    134
USA Networks, Inc., 141–142

Value-at-risk, 170
Value creation, 120
Value investing, 182
Value stocks, 109
Van, George, 53
Van Hedge Fund Advisors International:
    global hedge fund index, 53, 184
    international hedge fund index, 185
    U.S. hedge fund index, 54, 183

Vendex, 119
Vermut, Stephan, 59
Vickers, Marcia, 139
Vinik, Jeff, 84–85
Vivarte, 119
Volatility, 11, 103, 128, 142
Volcker, Paul, 90
Volkswagen, 120

Wald, Lillian, 38
Wall Street Journal, 56, 93, 117, 135
Weyerhaeuser Corporation, 119
Willamette Timber, 119
Williams, Mike, 102–108
Wong, Paul, 49–50, 176–177
World Bank, 46, 124
Wyser-Pratte, 113–123
Wyser-Pratte, Guy, 113–123, 138

Yield, 16